TRUE CRIME CASE HISTORIES - VOLUME 19

12 DISTURBING TRUE CRIME STORIES

JASON NEAL

JASON NEAL BOOKS

Cover images of:

Herbert Baumeister: (top-left)

Douglass Taylor: (top-right)

Lutz Kecke: (bottom-left)

Michele Kalina: (bottom-right)

More books by Jason Neal

Looking for more?? I am constantly adding new volumes of True Crime Case Histories. The series **can be read in any order**, and all books are available in paperback, hardcover, and audiobook.

Check out the complete series on Amazon series at:

https://geni.us/JasonNeal

FREE BONUS EBOOK FOR MY READERS

As my way of saying "Thank you" for reading, I'm giving away a FREE True Crime e-book I think you'll enjoy.

https://TrueCrimeCaseHistories.com

Just visit the link above to let me know where to send your free book!

INTRODUCTION

Evil doesn't always announce itself with warning signs.

Sometimes it lives quietly next door for years, sharing meals and small talk, until the day you discover what your neighbor was really doing in their basement. Sometimes it wears a uniform and a smile, using trust as a weapon. Sometimes it masquerades as love until the moment it decides you're disposable.

The twelve cases in this book represent a different kind of horror—not the random violence that makes headlines, but the calculated cruelty that festers in plain sight. These aren't crimes of passion or desperation. They're the methodical destruction of human life by people who had time to think, time to plan, and time to stop. They chose not to.

What you'll find here are stories where evil wore a familiar face.

•A devoted mother who transformed her family home into a burial ground.

•A delivery driver who decided a child's life was worth less than his job.

•Teenage girls who transformed jealousy into an eight-hour torture session.

•A state trooper who turned his badge into a hunting license for vulnerable young women.

•A couple who used their ordinary appearance to lure teenagers into unimaginable horror.

•A respected businessman who used the privacy of his sprawling estate to dispose of over twenty victims while maintaining his reputation in the community.

These perpetrators didn't snap; they revealed who they'd always been underneath the mask.

———

Some of these crimes took decades to solve, their victims forgotten until science finally caught up with justice. Others were solved quickly, but they left communities grappling with the realization that monsters don't always look like monsters. A few might make you reconsider how well you really know the people in your life.

Every detail in these stories is sourced through extensive research involving court records, police interviews, forensic reports, and witness testimony. While I occasionally reconstruct dialogue or protect certain identities, these horrors happened to real people who trusted the wrong person at the wrong moment. My aim is to honor their stories by telling them without filter or false comfort.

I won't sugarcoat what you're about to read. These stories don't have happy endings or redemptive conclusions. What you will find is the truth about what ordinary people can become when they stop pretending to be decent, as well as what happens to those unlucky enough to be nearby when the pretending ends.

These cases remind us that evil isn't an abstract concept or a distant threat. It's a choice that real people make, often while looking completely normal to everyone around them.

Many of these stories were recommended by readers who remembered cases from their communities or discovered them buried in local archives. If you know of a case that deserves attention, please keep those suggestions coming. The most chilling true crime stories are often the ones no one talks about anymore.

Additional photos, documents, and case materials can be found at: TrueCrimeCaseHistories.com/volume19

Welcome to the stories nobody wants to remember.

-Jason Neal

CHAPTER 1
THE VIKING PRINCESS

The yellow school bus wheezed to a stop on County Road 3573, its brakes squealing against the November afternoon quiet. Seven-year-old Athena Presley Strand bounced down the steps, her pink backpack sliding off one shoulder. She loved the color pink: pink clothes, pink toys, pink everything. Her family often joked that if something weren't pink, Athena would find a way to make it so.

Athena was the kind of child who filled rooms with her presence. Her teachers at school described her as bright and eager, always the first to raise her hand when a question was asked. She had an infectious smile that seemed to light up her entire face, and her laugh could make even the grumpiest adults crack a smile. When she talked about her future, she spoke with the absolute certainty that only children possess. She would be a Viking princess, she declared, complete with a pink helmet and armor.

Her creativity knew no bounds. At home, she would spend hours crafting elaborate stories about her imaginary adventures, often starring herself as the hero who saves kingdoms or discovers magical realms. She collected rocks from the yard, convinced that each one held special powers, and organized them by color and size in careful arrangements on her bedroom windowsill.

Paradise, Texas, lived up to its name in many ways. The small community in Wise County moved at a slower pace than the sprawling Dallas-Fort Worth metroplex just an hour south. Here, children still played outside until dark, neighbors knew each other's names, and the biggest worry most parents had was whether their kids finished their homework. This town had the kind of main street that looked like it belonged on a postcard, with local businesses that had been family-owned for generations and a courthouse square where residents gathered for summer festivals and Christmas parades.

Athena was spending this week with her father, Jacob Strand, and her stepmother at their home on a quiet county road. During the school year, she split her time between Texas and Oklahoma, where she lived with her mother, Maitlyn Gandy. However, this was a special visit; Thanksgiving had just passed, and Christmas was approaching. Athena had been chattering excitedly about what Santa might bring.

The afternoon of November 30, 2022, started like any other. Athena arrived home from school at 4:15 p.m., full of energy and stories from her day. Her stepmother was there to greet her, and the house settled into its usual after-school routine. Jacob, however, was away, having left earlier for a hunting trip in south Texas—a tradition he looked forward to each year.

As evening approached, a small disagreement erupted between Athena and her stepmother. Nothing serious, just the kind of minor conflict that happens in households with children every day. Athena, feeling upset, stepped outside to cool down. It was still light out, and the rural property offered plenty of safe space for a child to wander and think.

The stepmother continued with her evening tasks, keeping an ear out for Athena's return. Minutes passed. Then an hour. When she called for Athena and received no response, she stepped outside to look for her. The yard was empty. She checked the obvious places: behind the house, near the barn, around the vehicles parked in the driveway.

"Athena!" she called out into the growing dusk.

Silence.

At 6:40 p.m., she dialed 911.

"My stepdaughter is missing," she told the dispatcher, her voice tight with worry. "She went outside after we had a little argument, and I can't find her anywhere."

The call set in motion a response that would soon engulf the small community. Wise County Sheriff's deputies arrived within minutes, their patrol cars cutting through the rural quiet with flashing lights. Sheriff Lane Akin, a veteran lawman who had seen his share of difficult cases over the years, took personal command of the search.

Initially, the working theory was simple: A seven-year-old girl had wandered off after an argument and gotten lost in the rural landscape surrounding her home. It happened sometimes, especially with children who might be upset or distracted. The terrain around Paradise was a mix of open fields, patches of woodland, and winding creeks. Plenty of places for a small child to lose her way as darkness fell.

But as deputies began their systematic search of the property and surrounding areas, a nagging concern grew in the pit of Sheriff Akin's stomach. Athena's stepmother described her as a bright, responsible child who knew not to wander far from home, and the timing bothered him. It was getting cold, and even an upset seven-year-old would likely return home as temperatures dropped.

Word spread quickly through Paradise. By nightfall, hundreds of volunteers had materialized: neighbors, church members, relatives, and complete strangers who had heard about the missing child. They formed search lines and combed through fields with flashlights, calling Athena's name into the darkness. The local fire department brought ATVs and additional equipment. K-9 units arrived from neighboring counties, their handlers releasing the dogs to pick up any trace of the missing girl's scent.

From above, helicopters equipped with thermal imaging cameras swept back and forth across the landscape, their searchlights cutting through the night. The pilots looked for any heat signature that might indicate a small child huddled somewhere in the cold. Finally, drones joined the aerial search, their quiet humming adding to the symphony of desperate activity.

Jacob Strand received the call about his missing daughter while he was several hours away in South Texas. He immediately abandoned his hunting trip and began the frantic drive home, his mind racing through possibilities as mile after mile of dark highway passed beneath his headlights.

As Wednesday night stretched into Thursday morning, the initial optimism that Athena would be found safe began to waver. The search radius expanded from a few hundred yards around the house to a mile, then two miles, then five. Volunteer searchers, many of whom were parents themselves, pushed through exhaustion driven by the horrible knowledge that every passing hour decreased the chances of finding Athena alive.

Thursday brought new resources and new fears. The Texas Department of Public Safety arrived with additional personnel and equipment. FBI agents from the Dallas Field Office joined the investigation, bringing with them expertise in child abduction cases. The presence of federal agents sent a chill through the community. This was no longer just a search for a lost child; the FBI's Child Abduction Rapid Deployment (CARD) team brought specialized expertise into cases where time was critical. These agents had worked similar cases across the country, and their very presence carried an unspoken acknowledgment of what everyone feared but no one wanted to voice.

The command post near the Strand home had transformed into a hub of coordinated activity. Multiple agencies worked side by side, sharing information and resources in real time. Maps covered with grid patterns marked searched areas, while communications specialists maintained contact with search teams spread across miles of terrain. Volunteers continued to arrive throughout the day, some traveling from neighboring counties after hearing about the case via social media or local news.

Among the volunteers was Martha Henderson, a retired teacher who had driven thirty miles from Decatur after seeing Athena's photo on the news. "She reminded me of my own granddaughter," Henderson would later say. "I couldn't just sit at home knowing there was a little girl out there who needed help." Henderson joined a search line that methodically combed through a wooded area near a creek, calling Athena's name every few steps and listening intently for any response.

The emotional toll on the searchers was visible. Many were parents themselves, and every hour that passed without finding Athena brought them face to face with their own worst nightmares. Some had to step away periodically, overcome by the weight of what they were looking for. Others pushed through exhaustion, driven by a desperate hope that the next field, the next patch of woods, would yield the breakthrough everyone prayed for.

At 11:47 a.m. on December 1, an AMBER Alert flashed across cell phones, highway signs, and media outlets throughout Texas. Athena's photograph appeared alongside the details: a smiling girl with dark hair and bright eyes, missing since 5:40 p.m. the previous day from Paradise, Texas. The alert expanded the search beyond Wise County, enlisting millions of eyes across the state.

Sheriff Akin stood before a growing crowd of media and volunteers at a command post set up near the Strand home. His weathered face showed the strain of the past eighteen hours. He had been in law enforcement for decades, but cases involving children always hit harder.

"We are using every resource available to find Athena," he told the assembled crowd. "We will not stop until we bring her home."

But even as he spoke those words, investigators were beginning to piece together information that would transform the case from a missing child search into something far more sinister.

The family members themselves were cooperating fully with investigators, despite their emotional anguish. Jacob Strand, who had rushed home from his hunting trip, provided authorities with detailed information about his daughter's routines, her favorite hiding places, and anyone who might have had contact with her. Athena's stepmother walked investigators through the events of Wednesday evening multiple times, each retelling consistent with the last. Their openness and transparency helped investigators rule out family involvement early in the process, allowing them to focus their efforts elsewhere.

————

Deputies conducting door-to-door interviews in the area had learned something significant: A FedEx delivery had been made to the Strand home on Wednesday afternoon, around the time Athena had disappeared. The timing was too coincidental to ignore.

In the digital age, delivery companies like FedEx maintain detailed records of every package, every route, every stop. Investigators quickly obtained the delivery records for November 30. They learned that a package had been delivered to the Strand address at approximately 5:20 p.m., just twenty minutes before Athena was last seen.

The package contained Christmas gifts: Barbie dolls that had been ordered for Athena. The cruel irony wasn't lost on anyone involved in the investigation. Somewhere in the Strand home sat an unopened box of toys meant to bring joy to a little girl who might never get to play with them.

More importantly, the delivery records showed which driver had been assigned to that route. His name was Tanner Lynn

Horner, a thirty-one-year-old contract driver who worked for Big Topspin, Inc., a company that provided delivery services for FedEx.

As Thursday evening approached, investigators dug deeper into Horner's background. On the surface, nothing appeared particularly alarming. He lived in the Lake Worth area, near Fort Worth. He was engaged to be married and had a child of his own. Before driving for FedEx, he had worked as an Uber driver and maintained social media accounts that portrayed him as an aspiring musician living an ordinary life.

Tanner Lynn Horner

The ordinariness of Horner's background was perhaps the most unsettling aspect of all. This wasn't a case of an obvious predator with a long criminal history. Horner had passed the background checks required for his delivery job. He had interacted with hundreds, perhaps thousands of customers over the months he had been driving. His social media presence showed someone who appeared to be living a normal life, posting about his music, his relationship, and everyday concerns that millions of Americans shared.

His coworkers would later describe him as quiet but reliable. He showed up for his shifts on time, completed his routes efficiently, and never caused problems. The manager who had hired him remembered Horner as polite during his interview, as someone who seemed grateful for the opportunity to work. There had been no red flags, no warning signs that might have predicted what was to come.

But the digital trail was becoming impossible to ignore. GPS records from Horner's delivery truck placed him at the Strand residence at the crucial time. More significantly, investigators discovered that a neighbor's security camera had captured footage of a FedEx truck leaving the Strand property around the time Athena had vanished.

Late Thursday night, Sheriff Akin made the decision that would break the case wide open. Armed with this evidence, deputies located Horner's address in Lake Worth and began surveillance of his home. They watched and waited through the early hours of Friday morning, preparing for what they hoped would be the moment that brought Athena home safely.

As dawn broke on December 2, the truth finally emerged. Unfortunately, it wasn't the outcome anyone had prayed for.

———

At approximately 6:00 a.m., a convoy of law enforcement vehicles converged on Somerville Place Road in Lake Worth. Wise County deputies, Texas Rangers, and FBI agents surrounded Tanner Horner's residence. Neighbors peered out from their windows as officers pounded on the door of the modest home.

Horner answered, still in his sleepwear. The officers identified themselves and asked him to come with them for questioning about a missing child in Wise County. He didn't resist.

At the Wise County Sheriff's Office, Horner was placed in an interview room with experienced investigators. What happened over the next several hours would haunt everyone involved for years to come.

The interview room was stark and windowless, designed to eliminate distractions and focus attention on the conversation at hand. Experienced investigators led the questioning, drawing on years of training in interrogation techniques and criminal psychology.

Horner appeared nervous but cooperative. He answered initial questions about his work schedule and delivery route without hesitation. When asked specifically about the Strand residence, he readily admitted to making a delivery there on Wednesday evening.

It was when investigators pressed for more details about his time at the property that Horner's demeanor began to change. He shifted in his chair, his answers became shorter, and long pauses stretched between questions and responses. The detective, reading the subtle signs that came with decades of experience, sensed that they were approaching something significant.

According to Sheriff Akin's later statements, Horner's confession came relatively quickly. Faced with the mounting evidence against him, he admitted to taking Athena Strand, but the details he provided were far worse than anyone had imagined.

Horner told investigators that after delivering the package to the Strand home on Wednesday evening, he had been backing up his truck when he had accidentally struck Athena. The child, he claimed, was not seriously injured by the collision; she was conscious and able to speak. However, Horner said he'd panicked, consumed by the fear that Athena would tell her father about the accident.

In a decision that defied comprehension, Horner made a choice that would destroy multiple lives forever. Instead of helping the injured child or calling for medical assistance, he grabbed Athena and forced her into his delivery van.

The investigators listening to this confession struggled to maintain their professional composure. Here was a grown man describing, in matter-of-fact terms, how he had abducted a child to cover up an accident. The senselessness of it, the complete disproportion between the perceived problem and the solution, left detectives shaken.

The confession continued with more horrific details. Horner described attempting to break Athena's neck when she was in his van, and when that failed, strangling her with his bare hands. The child had pleaded for her life, he admitted, but he had not stopped. The clinical way he recounted these details, as if describing routine tasks rather than the torture and murder of an innocent child, chilled everyone in the room.

The lead detective would later say that, in all his years of law enforcement, he had never encountered a case where the motive seemed so utterly disconnected from the crime. Traffic accidents happened every day. Most resulted in insurance claims, sometimes minor injuries, and occasionally legal consequences. But murder? The killing of a seven-year-old child to avoid the inconvenience of reporting an accident? It defied comprehension.

Sheriff Akin, who observed the interview through a one-way window, felt something break inside him during those moments. He had been in law enforcement for decades, had worked cases involving domestic violence, drug-related murders, and other forms of human cruelty. Still, watching a man calmly describe strangling a seven-year-old girl was something that would stay with him for the rest of his life.

———

Horner's confession continued with the disposal of Athena's body. After killing her, he had driven around the rural areas of Wise County, eventually stopping at a remote creek along the Trinity River. There, approximately nine miles from her home, he had dumped Athena's body in the water.

By Friday afternoon, law enforcement vehicles were racing toward the location Horner had described. Sheriff Akin later said that the drive to that creek was one of the longest of his life, knowing what they would find but hoping against hope that somehow Horner was lying—that Athena might still be alive.

The convoy of vehicles wound through rural roads toward Boyd, Texas, a small community about nine miles from Paradise. The area Horner had described was remote, a spot along the Trinity River where fishermen sometimes came, but largely isolated from residential areas. It was the kind of place someone might choose if they wanted to ensure something wouldn't be found quickly.

As they approached the creek, the search team spread out along the banks. The water was shallow in most places, made murky by recent rains. Bare winter trees lined the waterway, their branches reaching across the narrow stream like gnarled fingers. It was a place of natural beauty that was about to become forever associated with unthinkable tragedy.

Deputies then spotted something in the water near a fallen log. At first, it was just a shape that didn't belong, but when they waded into the cold water for a closer look, their worst fears were confirmed.

The search team found her body in the shallow water, exactly where Horner had said it would be. Athena Presley Strand, who had been full of life and dreams just two days earlier, was dead.

———

At a press conference that evening, Sheriff Akin approached the podium with the weight of the world on his shoulders. He was a man who had delivered difficult news before, but never had the words felt so heavy. Behind him stood other members of law enforcement who had worked tirelessly on the case: Texas Rangers, FBI agents, and local deputies, all sharing in the collective heartbreak of the moment.

"It is with heavy hearts that we announce that the body of Athena Strand has been recovered," Akin began, his voice barely steady. He provided few details about the circumstances, citing the ongoing investigation, but confirmed that a suspect was in custody. As he spoke, the lights of the cameras seemed to burn into him, carrying his words to a community that had been holding its breath for two days.

Tanner Lynn Horner was formally charged with capital murder and aggravated kidnapping. His bond was set at $1.5 million, and he was placed in solitary confinement at the Wise County Jail.

The arrest brought an end to the search, but it marked the beginning of a new kind of anguish for Athena's family and community. Questions swirled about how something so horrific could happen in their quiet corner of Texas. How could a uniformed delivery driver, someone who was supposed to be trustworthy, commit such an unthinkable act?

As investigators continued their work, more disturbing details emerged. The Dallas County Medical Examiner's autopsy confirmed that Athena had died from blunt force injuries to the head and neck, combined with strangulation. Mercifully, there was no evidence of sexual assault. Horner's motive appeared to be exactly what he had claimed: a panicked attempt to silence a witness to his accident.

Even more troubling, police discovered that Horner faced unrelated charges for alleged sexual assaults of children dating back to 2013. These charges, filed in Tarrant County, raised questions about how someone with such a back-ground had been able to work as a delivery driver with access to people's homes.

———

Athena's father filed a wrongful death lawsuit against FedEx and Big Topspin, Inc., alleging that the companies had failed to properly screen and supervise their drivers. The civil case raised uncomfortable questions about corporate responsibility in an era when delivery drivers had become a constant presence in American neighborhoods. The lawsuit claimed that a more thorough background check might have revealed warning signs about Horner's character, particularly in light of the sexual assault charges that emerged after his arrest for unrelated incidents dating back to 2013.

FedEx responded by expressing sympathy for the family while maintaining that the company had followed proper hiring procedures. The corporate response highlighted a broader issue in the modern economy: As companies increasingly relied on subcontractors and independent drivers, the lines of responsibility for employee actions became blurred. The civil case was scheduled for trial in Dallas in mid-2025, ensuring that questions about corporate accountability would continue to be litigated long after the criminal proceedings concluded.

Perhaps more significantly, Athena's death sparked legislative action that would potentially save other children's lives. Texas lawmakers, moved by the circumstances of her disappearance, recognized a critical flaw in the existing AMBER Alert system. Because there had been no immediate evidence of abduction when Athena first went missing, the alert wasn't issued until nearly twenty-four hours after she disappeared. That precious time might have made a difference.

In May 2023, the Texas Legislature passed what became informally known as "Athena's Law." The new legislation created the "Athena Alert," a system that allowed local law enforcement to issue alerts for missing children even before all the strict AMBER Alert criteria were met. The law permitted alerts within a 100-mile radius when a child was believed to be in danger, potentially closing the gap that had delayed the initial alert for Athena.

Governor Greg Abbott signed the bill into law on June 13, 2023, with members of Athena's family present at the ceremony. For her parents, the law represented a bittersweet victory: a way to honor their daughter's memory while potentially preventing other families from experiencing similar anguish.

The legal proceedings against Horner moved forward with the methodical pace of capital punishment cases. In March 2023, he appeared in court to enter a formal plea of not guilty to both capital murder and aggravated kidnapping charges, despite his detailed confession to police. Athena's mother, Maitlyn Gandy, attended the arraignment. It was the first time she had been in the same room as the man accused of killing her daughter.

District Attorney James Stainton announced that prosecutors would seek the death penalty, a decision that required specialized legal representation for Horner. The case was eventually moved from Wise County to Tarrant County due to pretrial publicity, and the trial date was set for April 2026 after defense attorneys requested additional time to prepare.

Sheriff Lane Akin, the veteran lawman who had led the investigation, announced that the Athena Strand case would mark the end of his law enforcement career. The case, he said, had affected him more deeply than any other in his decades of service. He would never forget the moment when he'd had to tell Athena's parents that their daughter was dead, a moment that brought tears to his eyes even months later.

As the legal machinery continued to turn, processing the case through courts and appeals that could take years to resolve, the community of Paradise worked to heal while ensuring that Athena's memory lived on. On the first anniversary of her death, residents gathered at a memorial site near the creek where she was found, placing fresh pink flowers and sharing memories of a little girl whose life had been cut tragically short.

As the investigation concluded and the legal proceedings began, one image remained etched in the minds of everyone involved: a box of Barbie dolls, still unopened, sitting in the Strand home as a heartbreaking reminder of a Christmas that would never come for a little girl who had wanted to be a Viking princess when she grew up.

CHAPTER 2
THE WRONG CAR

The warm March air carried the sounds of college students celebrating another Friday night in Columbia's Five Points district. Neon signs flickered against brick buildings, casting colorful shadows on sidewalks crowded with University of South Carolina students. For twenty-one-year-old Samantha Josephson, this particular evening represented more than just another night out; it was a brief respite from the mounting pressures of senior year.

Samantha had every reason to feel optimistic about her future. The political science major from Robbinsville, New Jersey, had already secured a full scholarship to Drexel University's law school. Her dream of practicing international law felt within reach. She was weeks away from graduation, and tonight, surrounded by her Alpha Gamma Delta sorority sisters and friends, she allowed herself to simply be a college student enjoying the final chapter of her undergraduate experience.

———

The Bird Dog bar buzzed with its usual Friday night energy. Students clustered around high-top tables, their conversations mixing with the steady thrum of music. Samantha, with her warm smile and infectious laugh, moved happily among her friends. She had always possessed that rare quality of making others feel comfortable, of being genuinely interested in their stories and dreams.

As the night progressed and the crowd began to thin, Samantha made the decision that countless college students make every weekend. She was ready to head home. Her apartment wasn't far, but walking alone through Columbia's streets in the early morning hours wasn't something she wanted to risk. Like millions of young people across the country, she pulled out her phone and opened the Uber app.

At 2:09 a.m. on March 29, 2019, surveillance cameras outside the Bird Dog captured what appeared to be a routine moment. A young woman, phone in hand, approached a black Chevrolet Impala that had pulled up to the curb. The driver rolled down his window, presumably confirming the ride. Samantha, dressed in her going-out clothes and carrying her small purse, walked to the rear passenger door and climbed inside.

The car pulled away from the curb and disappeared into the darkness.

———

When Samantha's roommates woke up the next morning, they expected to find her sleeping in her own bed. Instead, they discovered an empty room and an unmade bed that hadn't been slept in. Phone calls went unanswered. Text messages remained unread.

By mid-morning, concern had transformed into genuine alarm. This wasn't like Samantha. She was responsible, reliable—the type of person who always let people know where she was going. Her boyfriend, Greg Corbishley, had been tracking her phone's location throughout the night, a common safety practice among college couples. The last ping had come from somewhere in Columbia's Rosewood neighborhood, then nothing.

Friends began retracing her steps from the previous evening. They confirmed she had left the Bird Dog alone, that she had called for an Uber, and that none of them had seen her get into any vehicle. The Uber driver who had been assigned to pick up Samantha came forward voluntarily. He had arrived at the designated location but never found his passenger. After attempting to call her several times, he had eventually canceled the ride.

By afternoon, Columbia police had officially opened a missing person investigation. The urgency was palpable—a young woman vanishing after a night out triggered every investigator's worst fears. Detective work began immediately, with officers canvassing the Five Points area and reviewing any available surveillance footage.

The security manager at the Bird Dog proved invaluable. The bar's external cameras had captured the exact moment Samantha had climbed into that black Chevrolet Impala. The footage was crystal clear: a young woman, alone and unsuspecting, getting into a car she believed would take her safely home.

But that wasn't her Uber.

———

Roughly sixty-five miles southeast of Columbia, in the rural expanse of Clarendon County, turkey hunters were making their way through wooded terrain near New Zion on the afternoon of March 29. The area was remote. It was the kind of place where locals might go to hunt or fish, but where strangers rarely ventured.

What they discovered in a secluded field would haunt them forever.

The body of a young woman lay partially concealed among the trees. Even from a distance, it was clear that something horrific had occurred. Blood had soaked through her clothing so thoroughly that the original colors were indiscernible. The hunters immediately contacted authorities, careful not to disturb what was obviously a crime scene.

Department of Natural Resources Officer Hendley Morris, who lived nearby, was among the first to respond. He secured the area until Clarendon County deputies and investigators from the South Carolina Law Enforcement Division (SLED) could arrive. The location was significant—remote enough that whoever had brought the body here knew the area well, yet accessible enough to reach by vehicle.

When investigators began processing the scene, the extent of the violence became clear. The victim had suffered massive trauma from what appeared to be multiple sharp-force injuries. Blood evidence suggested the attack had been prolonged and brutal. Personal items scattered nearby confirmed what everyone feared: This was Samantha Josephson.

———

News of the discovery sent shockwaves through Columbia and beyond. The University of South Carolina community reeled from the confirmation that one of their own had been murdered. For investigators, however, the real work was just beginning.

The surveillance footage from the Bird Dog became the key piece of evidence. The black Chevrolet Impala was clearly visible, and enhancing the video revealed distinguishing features of the vehicle. Like most cars in South Carolina, which only required rear license plates at the time, the Impala had no front plate to help with identification. Thus, investigators worked with what they could see—the vehicle's make, model, and partial rear plate information captured as it pulled away. A BOLO alert went out immediately to all law enforcement agencies in the region.

Columbia Police Detective investigators worked through the night, following up on any reported sightings of vehicles matching the description. The manhunt expanded as word spread through law enforcement networks. Every black Impala in the Columbia area became a potential lead.

Meanwhile, forensic experts began processing evidence from the crime scene in Clarendon County. The brutality of the attack was unlike anything many veteran investigators had encountered; the medical examiner's preliminary findings suggested the victim had suffered well over 100 separate stab wounds. The weapon appeared to be some type of blade or knife, and it had been wielded with extraordinary violence.

———

At 2:50 a.m. on March 30, just over twenty-four hours after Samantha had climbed into that black Impala, Columbia

Police Officer Jeffrey Kraft was patrolling the Five Points area when he spotted a vehicle that made him take notice.

A black Chevrolet Impala was making its way through the same area where Samantha had disappeared. The car matched the description from the BOLO alert, and when the driver made an illegal turn, Officer Kraft activated his emergency lights.

The traffic stop began routinely enough. Officer Kraft approached the vehicle and immediately detected the strong odor of marijuana emanating from inside. The driver, a young Black man, seemed nervous and claimed he didn't have his license with him. These were standard issues that officers dealt with regularly.

But then everything changed. Without warning, the driver bolted from the vehicle and took off running through the streets of Columbia, cutting through residential backyards and scrambling over fences in a desperate attempt to escape. Officer Kraft's dashcam and bodycam captured the sudden flight, the officer's pursuit, and his radio calls for backup. The foot chase wound through several blocks before Officer Justin Niscia intercepted the fleeing suspect and tackled him.

The man on the ground, breathing hard and struggling against the handcuffs, was twenty-four-year-old Nathaniel David Rowland.

Nathaniel Rowland

While Rowland was being processed and booked, investigators turned their attention to the abandoned Chevrolet Impala. What they found inside would provide the foundation for one of the most overwhelming murder cases in South Carolina's recent history.

Blood was everywhere.

The rear passenger seat, headrest, doors, and even the interior roof showed clear evidence of violent trauma. Blood spatter patterns suggested a prolonged struggle had taken place inside the confined space of the vehicle. The amount of blood was so extensive that anyone seeing it would immediately know something catastrophic had occurred.

But the blood was just the beginning.

Scattered throughout the vehicle were cleaning supplies: liquid bleach, germicidal wipes, window cleaner, and paper towels. Someone had clearly attempted to sanitize the interior, but the evidence of violence remained overwhelming.

On the front seat, investigators discovered a rose-gold iPhone. The phone's lock screen displayed a photo of a young woman who looked remarkably like Samantha Josephson. Nearby, they found a set of keys attached to a distinctive pink keychain—items that friends would later confirm belonged to Samantha. Among other papers in the vehicle, investigators also found an eviction notice that would play a key role in identifying Rowland's girlfriend, Maria Howard, leading them to additional evidence.

Perhaps most chilling was the discovery that the vehicle's child safety locks were engaged. These locks, controlled by a switch near the driver's seat, would have made it impossible for anyone in the back seat to open the doors from the inside. Samantha had been trapped.

As forensic technicians processed the vehicle, they noticed something else that told a heartbreaking story: footprint impressions on the inside of the rear windows. The prints appeared to have been made by someone desperately trying to kick their way out of the vehicle.

———

With Nathaniel Rowland in custody and overwhelming evidence connecting him to Samantha's disappearance, investigators began building their case. However, they needed more than just circumstantial evidence—they not only needed to establish how the crime had unfolded, but they also had to locate the murder weapon.

The answer came from an unexpected source: Rowland's girlfriend, Maria Howard.

Howard had witnessed Rowland's strange behavior in the hours following Samantha's murder, though she hadn't understood its significance at the time. She told investigators that Rowland had "slipped out" during the night, something he did frequently. When he'd returned the next morning, he was agitated and evasive.

Howard's most damning testimony involved what she had seen when she'd gotten into Rowland's car. Blood had covered the back seat near where her toddler's car seat was positioned. When she'd questioned Rowland about it, he had screamed at her to mind her own business. She'd also witnessed him meticulously cleaning the vehicle with bleach and scrubbing what appeared to be a knife.

Acting on this information, SLED agents obtained a search warrant for Howard's residence and the surrounding area. Searching trash containers behind her apartment, they made a discovery that would seal Rowland's fate.

Hidden among discarded household items was a multi-tool knife with two blades. The weapon was stained with what appeared to be blood, despite obvious attempts to clean it. Nearby, investigators found bloody rags, paper towels, cleaning wipes, and rubber gloves—all evidence of a desperate cleanup effort. They also discovered a black leather jacket with scratches across its surface, suggesting it may have been damaged during the struggle.

Also recovered were personal items belonging to Rowland that tested positive for blood, including clothing and a bandana. Most disturbing was a child's shoe belonging to Howard's daughter, stained with blood—evidence that the little girl had unknowingly come into contact with Samantha's blood when riding in the car. Had the garbage been collected on its regular schedule, most of this damning evidence would have been lost forever.

————

As laboratory results began coming back, the case against Nathaniel Rowland became overwhelming. DNA analysis confirmed that the blood found throughout his vehicle belonged to Samantha Josephson. The multi-tool knife recovered from the trash tested positive for both her blood and hair.

Fingerprint experts were able to match the heartbreaking footprints found on the interior windows of Rowland's car to Samantha's feet. Perhaps most revealing was a hand-written list found among Rowland's possessions. The note read like a sinister checklist: "duct tape, tape her whole body, gloves, all black, flip phone, gasoline, matches." The word "matches" had been crossed out, suggesting a change in plans.

Handwriting analysis confirmed the list had been written by Rowland himself, providing chilling evidence of premeditation. This wasn't a crime of opportunity. It had been planned.

Additional evidence emerged showing that Rowland had attempted to profit from his crime. ATM surveillance footage revealed someone matching his description trying to use Samantha's debit card to withdraw cash in the hours following her murder, though the person appeared to be deliberately concealing his face from the camera. Surveillance footage from a Columbia cell phone store showed Rowland attempting to sell a rose-gold iPhone— Samantha's—the morning after the murder.

————

The autopsy results confirmed the worst fears of everyone involved in the investigation. Dr. Thomas Beaver, the forensic pathologist, determined that Samantha had suffered approximately 120 separate stab wounds across her body.

The attack had been frenzied and brutal. Wounds covered her head, neck, shoulders, torso, back, arms, legs, and feet. Several injuries had penetrated vital organs and major blood vessels. One stab wound had gone completely through her right hand, evidence that she had tried desperately to defend herself. Another had penetrated her skull and entered her brain.

Most devastating was the discovery that Samantha's body contained only about twenty milliliters of blood—less than two tablespoons. The normal human body contains approximately four liters of blood. She had essentially bled to death from the massive trauma inflicted upon her.

Dr. Beaver estimated that Samantha had survived for only ten to twenty minutes after the attack began. The pattern of wounds suggested they had been inflicted by a double-bladed weapon in rapid succession, matching the multi-tool knife found in the trash behind Howard's apartment.

———

On July 20, 2021, more than two years after Samantha's murder, Nathaniel Rowland's trial began in Richland County. Judge Clifton Newman presided over proceedings that would lay bare one of the most heinous crimes in South Carolina's recent history.

The prosecution presented its case methodically. Over the course of a week, thirty-one witnesses testified, each adding another piece to the overwhelming puzzle of evidence against Rowland.

The turkey hunters who discovered Samantha's body described the horror of that March afternoon. Law enforcement officers recounted the traffic stop, the foot chase, and Rowland's arrest. Forensic experts walked the jury through DNA analysis, fingerprint comparisons, and blood spatter evidence.

Maria Howard's testimony proved particularly devastating. She described in detail Rowland's suspicious behavior, the blood in his car, and his efforts to clean up evidence. Her account provided the jury with a glimpse into the immediate aftermath of the crime and Rowland's callous response to having just committed murder.

The defense team, led by public defender Ashley Goode, faced an almost impossible task. The evidence against their client was overwhelming and irrefutable. Their strategy focused on highlighting the absence of Rowland's DNA on Samantha's body and the presence of an unidentified male DNA profile.

However, this approach failed to create reasonable doubt. Prosecutors effectively argued that Rowland had taken steps to avoid leaving biological evidence, including wearing gloves during the attack. The unknown DNA could be explained by any number of innocent contacts or contamination sources.

Most significantly, the defense called no witnesses, and Rowland himself chose not to testify. The jury never heard any explanation from the defendant about the overwhelming evidence against him.

On July 27, 2021, after deliberating for just over one hour, the jury returned with their verdict: guilty on all counts. Nathaniel Rowland was convicted of murder, kidnapping, and possession of a weapon during a violent crime.

The speed of the verdict reflected the strength of the prosecution's case. Jurors later indicated that the forensic evidence and timeline of events left no doubt about Rowland's guilt.

Judge Newman proceeded immediately to sentencing. Samantha's parents, Marci and Seymour Josephson, delivered emotional victim impact statements that brought many in the courtroom to tears.

Marci Josephson spoke of her recurring nightmares and the unbearable pain of visualizing her daughter's final moments. "I close my eyes and I feel what she endured at his hands, 120 times, over and over and over, fighting for her life, locked in his car," she said through tears.

Seymour Josephson described his overwhelming anger and guilt, his sleepless nights haunted by visions of his daughter's murder. He spoke of contemplating suicide, stopped only by concern for his wife and surviving daughter.

When given the opportunity to address the court, Rowland maintained his innocence. "I know I'm innocent, but I guess what I know and what I think doesn't really matter," he said, showing no remorse for Samantha's death.

Judge Newman, a veteran of the criminal justice system, called Rowland "heartless" and described the case as the most severe murder he had ever encountered. He sentenced Rowland to life in prison without the possibility of parole.

———

Samantha Josephson's murder sparked immediate action aimed at preventing similar tragedies. Her parents, rather than retreating into grief, channeled their pain into advocacy for rideshare safety.

The #WHATSMYNAME Foundation, established by Seymour and Marci Josephson, works to educate people about rideshare safety and has distributed thousands of safety cards to college students across the country. The foundation's central message is simple but potentially life-saving: Before getting into the vehicle, always ask your driver, "What's my name?"

Legislative action followed quickly. The Samantha L. Josephson Ridesharing Safety Act became law in South Carolina in June 2019, requiring rideshare vehicles to display front license plates and criminalizing the impersonation of rideshare drivers.

Similar laws, often called "Sami's Law," were enacted in New Jersey, North Carolina, and other states. At the federal level, legislation signed by President Biden in 2023 established national safety standards and created an advisory council to advance rideshare safety measures.

Uber and Lyft implemented additional safety features, including clearer displays of driver information and in-app safety tips. Universities across the country launched awareness campaigns, and the University of South Carolina established its own "#WhatsMyName" safety initiative.

———

Rowland's defense team filed appeals challenging various aspects of his conviction, including the legality of the traffic stop and the admission of certain evidence. However, in August 2024, the South Carolina Court of Appeals upheld all of Rowland's convictions.

The appellate court found that Officer Kraft had had reasonable suspicion to stop Rowland's vehicle, given that it matched the BOLO description and was spotted in the same area where Samantha had disappeared. Rowland's decision to flee on foot only strengthened the justification for the search of his vehicle.

The court noted that even if any individual piece of evidence had been improperly admitted, any such error would have been harmless given the "overwhelming evidence of guilt" against Rowland.

As of 2025, Nathaniel Rowland remains in prison serving his life sentence. His attempts at post-conviction relief have been unsuccessful, and he has exhausted his direct appeal options.

———

In May 2019, at what would have been her graduation ceremony, the University of South Carolina posthumously awarded Samantha Josephson her degree in political science. Her mother accepted the diploma on her behalf, a bittersweet moment that honored the bright future that had been stolen.

The Township of Robbinsville, New Jersey—Samantha's hometown—built a memorial patio and rock garden in her honor.

CHAPTER 3

BLUE EARTH JANE DOE

The telephone rang at 2:30 in the afternoon on May 9, 1980, cutting through the humid Texas air that hung heavy over Bay City. Don Busha Sr. answered with calloused hands, still dirty from his morning shift. The voice on the other end belonged to his daughter, Marla, and the worry in her tone made his stomach clench.

"Dad, when was the last time you heard from Michelle?"

The question hung between them like a prayer neither wanted to answer. Michelle had been calling home every week or two since she'd left in November, checking in first from Mississippi, then Indiana. Her voice always carried that mix of excitement and homesickness that tugged at her father's heart. But now, as Don counted backward through the days, he realized the calls had stopped.

"It's been three weeks," he said quietly.

That afternoon, Michelle Yvette Busha was officially reported missing.

———

Michelle's story had never been simple. Born November 2, 1961, she grew up in a household where the outside world felt forbidden and dangerous. Her Jehovah's Witness parents homeschooled her, creating a cocoon of isolation that left Michelle hungry for connection and adventure. The strict religious atmosphere clashed with her natural curiosity, and as she entered her teenage years, the tension became unbearable.

At seventeen, Michelle made her first escape. She ran to Colorado, seeking the freedom she'd dreamed about during long hours of Bible study and restricted social contact.

But the world beyond Bay City proved more treacherous than she'd imagined. In Burlington, Colorado, Michelle fell in with predatory individuals who saw vulnerability in the sheltered teenager. They drugged her, rendering her helpless and defenseless. Then they sexually assaulted her.

The assault shattered something fundamental in Michelle's understanding of the world. The freedom she had sought turned into a nightmare of violation and betrayal. When her father arrived to bring her home, he found a daughter forever changed by trauma. Michelle was wounded but not broken, carrying scars that would never fully heal, but determined not to let the experience define her entirely.

For a time, things improved. Living with her father and stepmother, Michelle found her footing. She made friends, something that had been nearly impossible in her isolated childhood, and she got a job at a local nursing home, where she cared for elderly residents who appreciated her gentle nature. The girl who had felt trapped began to bloom.

But the call of the road remained strong.

Shortly after her eighteenth birthday in November 1979, Michelle announced her plans. She and some friends were going to travel across the country, starting with Louisiana. This time, she wasn't running from something—she was running toward possibility.

Her family watched her go with a mixture of pride and terror.

———

Throughout the winter and into the spring, Michelle's voice traveled down telephone lines like a lifeline connecting her to Bay City. She called from Mississippi, her words painting pictures of small towns and new faces, then Indiana, where she spent time with people she'd met along the way.

Each call followed the same pattern. She would describe where she was, who she was with, and what she'd seen. Her family would update her on home—who had gotten married, who was sick, small-town gossip that meant everything when you were far away. Michelle always promised to call again soon.

"I'm okay," she would say before hanging up. "Don't worry about me."

But as April turned to May, the calls stopped coming.

———

As the years passed, Don Busha kept the same phone number, just in case. The family stayed at the same address, hoping that one day, Michelle would find her way home. They didn't realize that by the time they had reported her missing, she had already been dead for three days.

————

The rain had been falling for hours across southern Minnesota on May 30, 1980. Heavy spring storms turned dirt roads to mud and sent water rushing through ditches and drainage areas that normally ran dry. In Blue Earth, a small farming community near Interstate 90 with a population of just 3,000, the weather was simply another challenge in a season full of them.

A local farmer was checking his fields when he saw something that didn't belong among the corn stubble and prairie grass. At first, he thought it might be debris washed down by the storm, or maybe clothing or garbage thrown from a passing car. But as he got closer, the horrible truth became clear.

It was a body.

The young woman lay naked in the drainage ditch, her skin already showing signs of decomposition despite the cool spring weather. Her hair had been cut extremely short, leaving only a small patch at the back of her head. Most disturbing of all, her fingernails were completely missing. Not broken off, but removed entirely, as if someone had pulled them out with tools.

The farmer backed away and called the sheriff.

————

Faribault County Chief Deputy Jerry Kabe arrived at the scene within an hour of the call. A veteran investigator, he had worked plenty of difficult cases over the years, but the sight that greeted him in that Minnesota field was unlike anything he'd encountered.

The victim appeared to be a young woman, probably in her teens or early twenties. Caucasian, approximately 5'3", with brown hair that had been brutally shorn except for a small patch at the back of her head, her body showed clear signs of sexual assault and violence. The missing fingernails weren't about masking identity—it suggested torture. Around her neck, investigators found evidence of ligature strangulation. She had been killed with some kind of cord or rope.

But who was she?

The body carried no identification, no clothing, and no personal belongings of any kind. Someone had stripped her of everything that might reveal her identity. However, investigators did find some items nearby that initially seemed promising: blood-stained women's clothing and a driver's license lying on the ground. The license suggested the victim might have been from Texas, but forensic examination revealed the blood was animal blood, not human, and the driver's license was counterfeit—completely unconnected to the victim. These red herrings may have been coincidental trash or intentionally planted decoys, but they only added to the investigators' frustrations.

Kabe began the painstaking process of trying to match the victim to missing persons reports. He contacted law enforcement agencies across Minnesota, then expanded the search to neighboring states. Dental records were compared to missing persons cases in Colorado and Minnesota. Flyers were distributed nationwide, carrying the victim's description and a sketch of what she might have looked like in life.

Days turned to weeks. Weeks turned to months. No one came forward to claim her.

The young woman was buried in Riverside Cemetery in Blue Earth, in an unmarked grave labeled simply "Unknown."

————

In June 1988, eight years had passed when investigators at the Smith County Sheriff's Office in Texas received an unusual call. A Texas prison chaplain reported that an inmate in their custody—a former Minnesota state trooper named Robert Leroy Nelson—had been speaking about visions of harming someone in Minnesota during his patrol days.

Forty-two-year-old Nelson was serving two life sentences for the sexual assault of a minor. However, his comments about Minnesota caught the attention of investigators, who reached out to their colleagues up north.

Robert Leroy Nelson

When Minnesota detectives arrived at the Texas prison to interview Nelson, they found a man tormented by memories he could no longer suppress. At first, he spoke in vague terms, describing "visions of violence" along a Minnesota highway. However, as the interviews continued, the details became more specific and more chilling.

Nelson described picking up a young female hitchhiker near Interstate 90 in 1980. He said he was on duty, driving a marked patrol car, when he spotted her walking along the highway around 9:30 p.m. The girl had gotten out of a blue van after an argument, he claimed, and was trying to make her way west.

What happened next, Nelson confessed, was a crime of horrific brutality.

————

Robert Nelson's confession unfolded over several interviews, each session revealing new details that made investigators' stomachs turn. He described driving the hitchhiker to a secluded rural road, where he attempted to sexually assault her in the back of his patrol car. When she resisted and threatened to report him, Nelson said he "snapped."

He handcuffed the young woman to prevent her escape. He raped her repeatedly. Then, in an act of sadistic torture, he retrieved a pair of pliers from his trunk and systematically removed all ten of her fingernails while she was still alive and conscious.

The torture didn't end there. Nelson shaved off most of her hair, apparently to hinder identification. Finally, he took the drawstring from her own hooded sweatshirt and used it as a ligature, strangling her to death.

After killing her, Nelson meticulously destroyed evidence. He stripped the body completely, taking all clothing, jewelry, and personal belongings. He claimed he disposed of her clothes at a local landfill and hid her purse in a barn on a farm property he had been renting.

Then he dumped her naked body in a roadside drainage ditch and drove away.

Nelson insisted he never knew the victim's name. He said he believed she was traveling to Idaho or Oregon based on their brief conversation, but he had no identification for her. To him, she was just an opportunity that turned into a nightmare.

Questions Without Answers

Nelson's confession solved the question of who had killed the Blue Earth Jane Doe, but it left investigators with an even more frustrating mystery: Who was she?

In August 1989, Nelson pleaded guilty to first-degree manslaughter and was sentenced to eighty-six additional months in prison, to be served concurrently with his existing life sentences in Texas. The case was officially closed as far as the murder was concerned.

But in Riverside Cemetery, the grave still read "Unknown."

Jerry Kabe, the chief deputy who had worked the case from the beginning, found himself thinking about the nameless victim almost every day. "A murder like that doesn't leave your mind," he would say years later. "You live with it."

Somewhere, he knew, a family was still waiting for their daughter to come home.

———

In 2002, twenty-two years after the murder, a Blue Earth resident named Deborah Anderson was walking through Riverside Cemetery when she noticed the unmarked grave. A database manager by profession, Deborah was struck by the idea that someone could die and remain nameless, especially when the killer had already confessed.

Deborah began researching the case, reaching out to retired officers and digging through old newspaper reports. What she discovered frustrated her: Despite advances in DNA technology and the creation of national missing persons databases, no one had taken steps to enter the Blue Earth Jane Doe into these systems.

For over a year, Deborah lobbied local authorities to submit the case to the Minnesota Missing and Unidentified Persons Clearinghouse and the national NamUs database. She created a webpage for the case, commissioned an artist to create a facial reconstruction based on skull X-rays, and organized email campaigns to spread awareness.

Most importantly, she began advocating for something that had never been attempted: exhuming the body to collect DNA evidence.

———

By 2007, DNA technology had advanced to the point where even degraded samples from decades-old remains could yield useful profiles. That same year, in a development Deborah Anderson knew nothing about, Michelle Busha's family in Texas submitted their DNA samples to the FBI's Combined DNA Index System (CODIS).

Don Busha Sr. and his surviving family had never stopped looking for Michelle. Twenty-seven years after she went missing, they still hoped that science might provide the answer they'd been seeking.

Deborah's persistence finally paid off in 2014, when the Minnesota Bureau of Criminal Apprehension agreed to exhume the Blue Earth Jane Doe as part of their unidentified remains program. On August 12, 2014, thirty-four years after the murder, investigators carefully removed the remains from the unmarked grave.

Local businesses donated their services to keep costs minimal. A funeral home and construction companies performed the exhumation for free, leaving only $1,000 for DNA testing. The BCA crime lab was able to extract a viable nuclear DNA profile from the skeletal remains.

The profile was entered into CODIS and compared against thousands of family reference samples from across the country.

―――――

On March 5, 2015, the computer found a match.

The DNA from the Blue Earth Jane Doe matched samples submitted by the Busha family eight years earlier. Dental records were cross-referenced to confirm the identification. After thirty-five years, the nameless victim finally had her identity restored.

The Blue Earth Jane Doe was Michelle Yvette Busha of Bay City, Texas.

―――――

At a news conference on March 17, 2015, Faribault County Sheriff Mike Gormley announced the identification to a room full of reporters and investigators. Some of the officers present had worked the original case. Jerry Kabe, now retired, was there to see the conclusion of the mystery that had haunted him for decades.

"We have some answers after thirty-five years of waiting," said Catherine Knutson, director of BCA Forensic Science Services. "We know who she is."

Michelle's family, shocked to learn she had been in Minnesota at all, was finally able to bring their daughter home. They had maintained the same phone number and address for years, hoping she would reach out. Instead, science had delivered the call they'd been waiting for.

———

In April 2015, Michelle's remains were cremated and released to her family. The girl who had left Bay City seeking adventure, who had called home faithfully until those calls suddenly stopped, was finally coming back to Texas.

Deb Anderson, the woman whose twelve-year campaign had made the identification possible, described the resolution as bittersweet. She had spent over a decade fighting for a stranger, advocating for someone she had never met but whose story had captured her heart.

"I mourned her," Deb said. "I felt like I knew her."

The case highlighted the thousands of unidentified remains across the country—the FBI estimates there are over 10,000 "Jane and John Does" nationwide, with Minnesota alone maintaining seventy other ongoing cases. Michelle's identification demonstrated both the power of modern forensic science and the importance of citizen advocacy when official resources fall short.

Robert Leroy Nelson remains in a Texas prison, where he continues to serve his life sentence. Now in his late seventies, he has been denied parole repeatedly, with his next review scheduled for 2027. Deb Anderson has made it her mission to ensure he never goes free, participating in parole hearings and organizing opposition to his release.

"This will probably go on until he dies," she said. "I'll be doing this for a while."

————

Michelle Busha's grave in Texas now bears her real name. The teenager who ran away seeking freedom, who called home faithfully until the calls stopped, who trusted a uniformed officer who betrayed that trust in the most horrific way possible, is no longer an unknown victim.

Her story serves as a reminder of both the dangers faced by vulnerable young people and the power of persistence in seeking justice. It took thirty-five years, advances in DNA science, and the unwavering dedication of a stranger who refused to let her remain nameless.

Jerry Kabe, the investigator who worked the case from the beginning, finally found the closure that had eluded him for decades. The nightmare that had followed him through retirement was over.

"It's something that never leaves your mind," he reflected. "I've thought about her almost every day."

But now, at least, he knew her name.

CHAPTER 4

THE HOUSE ON CHIPMAN STREET

The dinner had been perfect. Channon Christian, twenty-one and radiant in the way that comes naturally to college seniors who believe the world holds endless possibilities, sat across from her boyfriend at their favorite Knoxville restaurant. Christopher Newsom, twenty-three, with calloused hands that spoke of his work as a carpenter and eyes that lit up whenever he looked at her, reached across the table to squeeze her fingers.

They had been together for several months, and Chris had already started talking about the future in that careful way young men do when they're testing the waters. Channon, a sociology major at the University of Tennessee who was set to graduate in just a few months, would laugh and change the subject, but friends noticed she never pulled her hand away when he reached for it.

That Saturday evening, January 6, 2007, they had plans after dinner. A friend was throwing a birthday party, and they had promised to stop by. Channon drove her silver Toyota 4Runner through the familiar streets of Knoxville, a city where she had spent most of her twenty-one years and felt completely safe. Chris sat in the passenger seat, occasionally reaching over to adjust the radio or point out something interesting along the way.

At 8:00, they pulled into the parking lot of the Washington Ridge apartment complex. The party was upstairs, but Chris wanted to say something first. He stepped out of the vehicle and walked around to the driver's side, leaning down to kiss Channon through the open window. She laughed at something he whispered, her face illuminated by the parking lot lights.

Neither of them noticed the shadows moving between the cars.

The attack came without warning. Multiple figures emerged from the darkness, weapons drawn, shouting commands. Within moments, both Channon and Chris found themselves forced into the backseat of her own SUV, their hands bound, their voices silenced by the cold reality of gun barrels pressed against their heads.

The 4Runner pulled out of the parking lot and disappeared into the Knoxville night.

————

Gary and Deena Christian awoke on Sunday morning expecting a call from their daughter. Channon was responsible about checking in, especially when she stayed out late. When the phone remained silent and their calls went straight to voicemail, concern crept in like cold water rising.

By afternoon, that concern had transformed into panic.

Hugh and Mary Newsom were experiencing the same terrible awakening. Their son Chris, reliable as the sunrise, had not come home. His phone went unanswered. His friends hadn't seen him since the previous evening.

The families began making calls. Had anyone seen Channon and Chris? When was the last time someone had spoken to them? The answers painted a picture that made no sense: The couple had planned to attend a birthday party but never arrived. Their friends had waited, then assumed they had changed their minds. No one had thought to worry until the families had started asking questions.

By Sunday afternoon, both families had attempted to file missing persons reports but were told by the Knoxville Police Department that, since they were both adults, they would need to wait at least twenty-four hours.

———

The call came in at 12:20 p.m. on Sunday, January 7. A railroad employee working the tracks near Ninth Avenue and Cherry Street in East Knoxville had spotted something that shouldn't have been there.

Officers arrived at the scene and climbed the embankment, following the railroad worker's directions, and found themselves staring at something that would haunt them for years to come.

The body of a young man lay alongside the tracks, partially burned and still smoldering. The victim was bound hand and foot, blindfolded with what appeared to be a bandana, and gagged with a sock secured by a shoelace wrapped around his head. Even in death, the restraints told a story of unimaginable terror.

The officers immediately called for backup and the medical examiner. As more officers arrived, they began processing the crime scene. The victim's feet were bare and covered in mud, suggesting he had walked to this location. His clothing was minimal and showed signs that he had been sexually assaulted. He was found naked from the waist down.

The medical examiner arrived on the scene and conducted a preliminary examination that revealed three gunshot wounds: one to the back, one to the neck, and a fatal shot to the head above the right ear that had severed the brain stem. The body had been doused with gasoline and set ablaze after death.

The victim's wallet was missing, but other identifying factors quickly led investigators to a devastating conclusion. This was Christopher Newsom, the young man whose family was desperately searching for him. But one urgent question still loomed: If Chris was dead, then where was Channon?

————

Gary Christian couldn't sit still. While police processed the crime scene and began their investigation into his daughter's boyfriend's murder, Gary took to the streets of Knoxville with the desperate energy of a man who refused to accept the worst.

He drove through neighborhoods, stopping to ask anyone he saw if they had noticed a silver Toyota 4Runner. He posted flyers with Channon's photograph on telephone poles and storefront windows. He called his daughter's friends and did his best to retrace her movements from the previous evening.

On Monday morning, January 8, Gary's persistence paid off in a way that would break his heart, but also break the case wide open.

Driving slowly through the area near where Chris's body had been found, Gary spotted a familiar vehicle parked on Glider Avenue, just a few blocks from the railroad tracks. The silver Toyota 4Runner sat empty, its doors unlocked, appearing to have been hastily abandoned.

Gary immediately called the police, who rushed to secure the vehicle. Crime scene technicians spent hours processing the SUV, collecting fingerprints, fibers, and any other evidence that might lead them to Channon. The vehicle had been wiped clean in most places, but investigators managed to lift one clear fingerprint from a bank envelope found inside.

That fingerprint would change everything.

———

Investigators had worked hundreds of cases during their years with the Knoxville Police Department, but few had generated the intensity surrounding the search for Channon Christian. With her boyfriend's tortured body found alongside railroad tracks and her vehicle abandoned nearby, everyone involved knew they were racing against time.

The fingerprint recovered from Channon's SUV was rushed to the Tennessee Bureau of Investigation's crime lab. By Monday evening, January 8, the results came back with stunning clarity.

The print belonged to Lemaricus Devall Davidson, a twenty-five-year-old ex-convict with a history of carjacking and robbery. Davidson had been released from prison just months earlier after serving time for violent crimes. Even more significantly, Davidson's last known address was 2316 Chipman Street. That was less than half a mile from where the SUV was found and Chris's body was discovered.

Lemaricus Devall Davidson

Investigators felt the familiar surge of adrenaline that came with a breakthrough. They had a name, an address, and a clear connection to the victims' vehicle, but they still didn't have Channon.

As Monday night turned into Tuesday morning, investigators prepared to obtain a search warrant for Davidson's residence. They had no way of knowing what they would find there, but every hour that passed without locating Channon decreased the likelihood that she was still alive.

———

A search warrant was issued at 1:00 p.m. on Tuesday, January 9. By 1:30 p.m., a team of Knoxville police officers and FBI agents was standing outside the small, one-story rental house at 2316 Chipman Street.

The neighborhood was quiet, typical of working-class East Knoxville. The house itself appeared unremarkable—white siding, small front porch. Nothing to suggest the horrors that had unfolded inside just days earlier.

Officers approached the front door while others positioned themselves around the perimeter. The house appeared empty, but they couldn't be certain until they cleared each room.

The front door was unlocked.

Inside, the house showed signs of recent occupancy but current abandonment. Fast food containers and empty bottles were scattered across surfaces. Clothing was strewn about as if the occupants had left in a hurry. However, it was the evidence of violence that immediately caught the investigators' attention.

Bloodstains on the carpeting. Torn fabric. Personal items that clearly didn't belong to whoever lived in the house.

Investigators made their way toward the kitchen, following their instincts and the subtle guidance of the crime scene technician who had begun documenting everything with photographs. That's when they saw the large residential garbage can sitting in the corner.

Something was wrong with it. The can was too full, and there were what appeared to be black garbage bags protruding from the top. But there was also something else—a floral pattern that looked like bedding material.

The officers called for the medical examiner before opening the container. The medical examiner arrived within thirty minutes, and together, they carefully removed the bags and fabric from the garbage can.

What they found inside would haunt everyone present for the rest of their lives.

———

Channon Christian's body was bound in a fetal position, wrapped in multiple black garbage bags, and secured with strips of bedding. She had been severely beaten, and chemical burns around her mouth and genital area indicated that bleach had been poured on her, apparently in an attempt to destroy DNA evidence.

The medical examiner's preliminary examination revealed extensive trauma consistent with prolonged sexual assault. Channon had been brutally gang-raped multiple times, vaginally, orally, and anally. The positioning of her body within the garbage can, combined with the tight binding around her head and the plastic bags, told a horrific story.

Channon Christian had been left to die slowly, suffocating in that trash can while bound and unable to move.

The medical examiner estimated that death had occurred sometime late on January 7 or early January 8, meaning Channon had survived for nearly two full days after the initial abduction, enduring unimaginable torture before finally succumbing to positional asphyxia.

As crime scene technicians continued processing the house, they found additional evidence that played a key role in identifying and prosecuting those responsible. Personal items belonging to both victims were scattered throughout the house, while DNA evidence would later link multiple perpetrators to the crimes. And perhaps most damning of all, investigators found clear signs that this had been no random crime or drug deal gone wrong.

This had been a prolonged, intentional campaign of torture and murder.

———

The evidence found at 2316 Chipman Street painted a picture of multiple attackers, but Lemaricus Davidson's fingerprint in Channon's vehicle made him the primary target of the manhunt that immediately followed.

Investigators quickly learned that Davidson had not been living alone at the Chipman Street house. Witnesses in the neighborhood reported seeing several people coming and going from the residence over the weekend, including Davidson's half-brother Letalvis Cobbins, a friend named George Thomas, and a young woman later identified as Vanessa Coleman.

The investigation also revealed that Davidson had reached out to another friend, Eric Boyd, for help after the murders. Phone records and witness statements suggested that Boyd had assisted Davidson in hiding out after the crimes were committed.

By Wednesday, January 11, law enforcement agencies across multiple states were coordinating efforts to apprehend the suspects. The break came when Kentucky authorities located Cobbins and Thomas at a friend's house in Lebanon, just outside Louisville. When officers moved in to make the arrests, they found the two men in possession of items that had belonged to Channon Christian.

That same day, federal marshals and Knoxville police tracked Davidson to an empty house on Reynolds Street in Knoxville. When the SWAT team breached the door, they found Davidson hiding inside. He was wearing Christopher Newsom's Nike athletic shoes.

As officers placed him under arrest, Davidson's first words were a denial that would prove prophetic in its specificity: "I didn't do anything to that girl."

The arrests of Davidson, Cobbins, and Thomas provided investigators with the opportunity to piece together exactly what had happened during those terrible three days in January. Through interviews, physical evidence, and witness statements, a horrific timeline began to emerge.

————

The carjacking at Washington Ridge had been a crime of opportunity. Davidson and his associates had been in the area, likely looking for potential victims, when they had spotted Channon and Chris in the parking lot. The couple's obvious affection for each other, their nice vehicle, and their apparent prosperity had made them attractive targets.

After forcing the couple into the SUV at gunpoint, the attackers had driven them back to Davidson's rental house on Chipman Street. There, over the course of several hours, both victims had been subjected to brutal sexual assault and torture.

Christopher Newsom had been taken from the house early on January 7, likely by Davidson and Eric Boyd. He had been forced to walk barefoot to the nearby railroad tracks, where he was bound, blindfolded, and gagged before being executed with three gunshots. His body was then doused with gasoline and set on fire.

Channon Christian had remained at the house, where she endured continued sexual assault by multiple attackers. The medical evidence suggested she had been raped repeatedly over a period of many hours. She had been beaten severely, and her attackers had poured bleach over her body and into her mouth and genitals, apparently believing this would destroy DNA evidence.

Finally, Channon had been bound with strips of bedding, her head had been covered with plastic bags, and she'd been shoved into the garbage can, where she had slowly suffocated.

What made the crimes even more chilling was the casual indifference displayed by the perpetrators afterward. Evidence showed that Davidson had left the house on January 7, while Channon was likely still alive in the garbage can, to visit an ex-girlfriend. He had given away some of Channon's personal belongings and had worn Chris's shoes during this social call, as if nothing had happened.

———

While Davidson, Cobbins, and Thomas were in custody by January 11, investigators knew their work wasn't complete. Eric Boyd, who had helped Davidson hide after the murders, was arrested on January 12 on federal charges of being an accessory after the fact.

The final arrest came on January 31, when Vanessa Coleman was taken into custody in Lebanon, Kentucky. The eighteen-year-old had initially been questioned and released when Cobbins and Thomas were arrested, but as evidence mounted and her role in the crimes became clearer, authorities obtained warrants for her arrest as well.

Coleman's case would prove particularly disturbing when investigators discovered diary entries she had written in the days immediately following the murders. Rather than expressing horror or remorse at what she had witnessed, Coleman had written about having "one helluva adventure in Tennessee" and expressed enthusiasm about her life.

By early February 2007, all five individuals connected to the murders were in custody, facing charges. A Knox County grand jury returned a forty-six-count indictment against Davidson, Cobbins, Thomas, and Coleman, including charges of first-degree murder, felony murder, especially aggravated robbery, especially aggravated kidnapping, aggravated rape, and theft.

Eric Boyd was initially prosecuted only in federal court for his role in helping Davidson evade arrest, though his involvement in the actual murders would become the subject of a renewed investigation more than a decade later.

———

Eric Boyd was the first to face trial, appearing in federal court in April 2008 on charges of being an accessory after the fact. The prosecution painted a horrific picture for the jury, describing how Channon was gang-raped, penetrated with objects, choked, stomped on, and bound. She was then put into the trash can while still alive. The prosecutor detailed how Chris had been "sodomized, shot in the back, shot in the neck, and… a kill shot to his head," then doused with gasoline and burned. Boyd was convicted and sentenced to eighteen years in federal prison.

The state trials began in earnest in 2009 under Judge Richard Baumgartner. Letalvis Cobbins was tried first, with a jury brought in from Nashville due to the extensive local publicity. In August 2009, the jury convicted Cobbins on thirty-three charges, including the first-degree murder of Channon Christian. He was sentenced to life in prison without the possibility of parole.

Lemaricus Davidson's trial followed in October 2009. As the alleged ringleader, Davidson faced the most serious charges. The evidence against him was overwhelming: his fingerprints in Channon's SUV, his semen recovered from her body, and witness testimony placing him at the scene. Davidson was found guilty on all forty-six counts, including the premeditated murder of both victims. The jury unanimously recommended the death penalty, and Davidson was sentenced to death by lethal injection.

George Thomas was tried in December 2009 in Hamilton County. Despite his defense's claims that he was merely present and not an active participant, the jury convicted him on all charges related to both murders. He received two consecutive life sentences without the possibility of parole.

Vanessa Coleman, tried last in May 2010, faced a somewhat different case. At eighteen at the time of the crimes, she was not charged with directly causing the deaths. However, prosecutors introduced devastating evidence from her own journal, where she had written about having "one helluva adventure in Tennessee" just days after the murders. The jury convicted her on thirteen of seventeen counts, including facilitation of murder, rape, and kidnapping. She was sentenced to fifty-three years in prison.

————

Just as it seemed justice had been served, a shocking revelation would throw the entire case into chaos. In early 2011, Judge Richard Baumgartner, who had presided over all the state trials, was discovered to have been battling a prescription drug addiction throughout the proceedings.

The Tennessee Bureau of Investigation revealed that Baumgartner had been improperly obtaining opioids and was sometimes impaired on the bench. He had even purchased pills from a felon who had appeared in his court. In March 2011, Baumgartner pleaded guilty to official misconduct and resigned from the bench.

The scandal sent shockwaves through the legal system. Defense attorneys for all four defendants immediately filed motions for new trials, arguing that Baumgartner's compromised state had denied their clients fair proceedings. In December 2011, Judge Jon Kerry Blackwood granted new trials for all four defendants. This devastated the victims' families, who had thought their ordeal was over.

The state appealed, and in May 2012, the Tennessee Supreme Court partially overturned Blackwood's decision. The court ruled that Davidson and Cobbins would not receive new trials, as there was no evidence that Baumgartner's condition had actually affected their proceedings. However, the court allowed new trials for Thomas and Coleman, finding that Baumgartner had appeared particularly impaired during Coleman's sentencing.

The legal proceedings stretched on for years. Vanessa Coleman was retried in November 2012 and again convicted on multiple charges, but this time, she was sentenced to only thirty-five years—a reduction from her original fifty-three-year term.

George Thomas was retried in May 2013, once again convicted on all charges, and sentenced to two consecutive life sentences. His new sentence technically allowed for the possibility of parole after fifty-one years, meaning he could potentially be released while in his seventies.

More than a decade after the original crimes, investigators developed new evidence against Eric Boyd. He was indicted on state charges in 2018, including first-degree murder, with testimony from George Thomas implicating Boyd more directly in the actual killings. In August 2019, a Knox County jury found Boyd guilty on nearly all charges. He was sentenced to two consecutive life sentences plus ninety years, ensuring he would never be released.

As of today, Lemaricus Davidson remains on Tennessee's death row, his appeals exhausted. Letalvis Cobbins serves life without parole. George Thomas continues serving his life sentence with the remote possibility of parole decades in the future. Vanessa Coleman has been repeatedly denied parole, most recently in 2020, with her next hearing scheduled for 2030. Eric Boyd will spend the rest of his life in prison.

―――――

The murders of Channon Christian and Christopher Newsom sent shockwaves through Knoxville and beyond. The random nature of the crime, two young people simply in the wrong place at the wrong time, shattered the sense of security that many residents had taken for granted.

Gun permit applications surged in the weeks following the murders, particularly among women. Residents who had never thought twice about walking to their cars alone at night suddenly found themselves looking over their shoulders. Parents began having conversations with their college-age children about situational awareness and personal safety.

―――――

The case also sparked intense debate about media coverage and racial dynamics. The brutal nature of the crimes, combined with the fact that the victims were white and all five perpetrators were Black, drew attention from various groups seeking to exploit the tragedy for their own agendas. On May 28, 2007, a white supremacist group held a protest in Knoxville, alleging that the case was being deliberately downplayed by national media because it didn't fit the preferred narrative of white-on-Black crime. The protest claimed that if the racial roles had been reversed, the story would have dominated national headlines.

However, this demonstration was met with significant community opposition. Local residents, law enforcement officials, and most importantly, the victims' families themselves firmly rejected any attempt to turn their loved ones' deaths into a racial rallying cry. Investigators and prosecutors consistently emphasized that the crimes stemmed from the perpetrators' criminal intent and history of violence, not racial motivation. The consensus among law enforcement was that this had been a random crime of opportunity. Channon and Chris were simply in the wrong place at the wrong time, targeted because they appeared vulnerable and prosperous, not because of their race.

Both the Christian and Newsom families repeatedly and forcefully rejected any racist exploitation of their children's deaths, focusing instead on honoring Channon and Chris's memory while ensuring that justice was served through the legal system.

———

What remained undisputed was the profound impact on the families of the victims. Gary Christian, who had maintained his composure throughout the search for his daughter, finally broke down when confronted with the reality of what she had endured. In the weeks that followed, he expressed intense anguish and anger, initially turning away from God before later finding faith again.

Hugh and Mary Newsom faced their own journey through grief, trying to reconcile the memories of their son's gentle nature with the violence of his final hours. Both families would eventually channel their pain into advocacy for victims' rights and criminal justice reform, but that process would take years.

The victims' families attended hundreds of court proceedings over more than a decade, never wavering in their pursuit of justice for Channon and Chris. Their persistence led to changes in Tennessee law—the Channon Christian Act and Chris Newsom Act—designed to protect future victims and prevent the legal complications that had plagued their case.

The house on Chipman Street was eventually demolished, but the memories endure in the hearts of a community that learned evil could strike anywhere, at any time.

CHAPTER 5
THE LIMBURG SCHOOLGIRL MURDERS

The music pounded through the speakers at the discotheque named "Anyway" in Elz, Germany, as teenagers packed the dance floor on what seemed like any other Saturday night in October 1994. Among the crowd, two sixteen-year-old best friends from Limburg-Blumenrod moved through the haze of cigarette smoke and flashing lights, their laughter mixing with the thumping bass that vibrated through the floor.

Jasmin G. and Yvonne H. had been inseparable since childhood. Both girls shared the same infectious energy that drew others to them—Jasmin with her quick wit and mischievous grin, Yvonne with her gentle nature and ready smile. They had spent the evening bouncing between nightclubs, starting at a discotheque in Diez before making their way to the popular "Anyway" club. The night felt endless with possibility, the way nights do when you're sixteen and the world stretches out before you.

As the clock crept past 3:00 a.m. on October 9th, the crowd began to thin. The girls found themselves in the parking lot outside the club, saying goodbye to friends who were heading home. The autumn air carried a chill that made them pull their jackets tighter as they looked around for a ride back to Limburg.

That's when they encountered the couple.

A woman approached them with a friendly smile, asking if they needed a lift home. She seemed harmless enough—middle-aged, with the kind of maternal presence that put the girls at ease. Her husband waited nearby, quiet but not threatening. After a brief conversation, Jasmin and Yvonne climbed into the car.

The vehicle pulled away from the club's parking lot and disappeared into the German countryside. By dawn, when their families expected them home, both girls had vanished without a trace.

———

The first calls came early on Sunday morning. Jasmin's mother dialed Yvonne's house, her voice tight with worry. Neither girl had returned home, and their beds remained untouched. The families tried to remain calm—perhaps the girls had stayed over at a friend's house, or maybe they'd lost track of time. But as the hours stretched on and phone calls to every friend turned up nothing, a cold dread settled over both households.

Jasmin lived with her mother in a modest apartment in Limburg-Blumenrod, their relationship close despite the typical teenage tensions. Her mother worked long hours to support them both, but she made sure to check on Jasmin whenever she went out. Yvonne came from a larger family, with siblings and parents who doted on their bright, ambitious daughter.

By Sunday evening, when still no word had come, both families contacted the police.

The initial response was measured. Sixteen-year-old girls sometimes stayed out longer than planned, especially after a night of clubbing. However, the officers who took the reports noted something troubling: Both girls were described as good students and reliable, the type who always called if they were going to be late. Their disappearance felt different from typical teenage rebellion.

As the days passed with still no sign of either girl, the investigation began.

———

Detective Inspector Klaus Müller had worked missing persons cases for over a decade, but something about this one gnawed at him from the start. Two girls disappearing together wasn't unheard of, but the complete absence of any trace was unusual. No abandoned belongings, no witnesses after they left the club, no activity on any identification they might have carried.

The investigation team began reconstructing the girls' final hours. They interviewed dozens of clubbers who had been at Disco Anyway that night, searching for anyone who might have seen them leave or noticed who they left with. The club's parking lot offered no obvious clues—too many cars had come and gone, obliterating any useful tire tracks or evidence.

One witness remembered seeing the girls talking to an older couple near the parking area, but the description remained frustratingly vague. A woman, perhaps in her thirties or forties, with dark hair. A man, average height, nothing particularly distinguishing about him. The witness couldn't recall the type of car or even its color with certainty.

The detectives expanded their search, checking hospitals throughout the region in case the girls had been in an accident. They contacted train stations and bus terminals, wondering if perhaps the teenagers had decided to run away together. Every lead seemed to evaporate upon closer examination.

As the days became a week, the mood in both families shifted from worry to something approaching panic. Jasmin's mother barely slept, pacing their small apartment and calling everyone she could think of. Yvonne's parents organized search parties, combing the woods and fields around Limburg with friends and neighbors.

The police deployed search dogs and brought in volunteers to help cover more ground. However, the countryside around Limburg stretched for miles in every direction, offering countless places where two girls might be hidden— or where something terrible might have happened to them.

Then came the call that changed everything.

———

Wilhelm Schneider had been cutting timber in the forests near Hüttenberg-Volpertshausen for twenty-three years. He knew every path, every clearing, every stack of logs in his section of the woods. So when he arrived at his usual spot behind a large pile of timber on the morning of October 11, he immediately noticed something that didn't belong.

At first, he thought someone had dumped old mannequins or clothing. As he approached with his customer, a local man who had come to purchase firewood, the horrifying reality became clear.

Two naked bodies lay on the forest floor, pale and still in the morning sunlight filtering through the trees. Neither man moved closer. Schneider felt his legs go weak as the full horror of what they were seeing sank in.

The two men backed away from the scene, careful not to disturb anything, and hurried back through the forest to Schneider's truck. The drive to the nearest house with a telephone felt endless, though it took only ten minutes to reach the small farmhouse where Schneider's neighbor lived. With trembling hands, he dialed the emergency number while his customer sat in stunned silence on the front steps.

Within an hour, the quiet forest clearing had transformed into a crime scene buzzing with activity. Police cars lined the narrow dirt road leading to the timber pile, their blue lights flashing uselessly in the daylight. Detective Müller arrived to find the area already cordoned off with yellow tape, uniformed officers keeping back a small crowd of curious neighbors drawn by the commotion.

The first thing that struck him was the remoteness of the location. This wasn't a spot someone would stumble upon by accident. Whoever had brought the bodies here knew the area well, had chosen this place specifically for its isolation. The killer wanted the bodies found eventually, but not too soon.

Dr. Elisabeth Hoffman from the Institute of Legal Medicine in Gießen arrived to conduct the preliminary examination. A veteran forensic pathologist with steel-gray hair and wire-rimmed glasses, she had seen enough violent death to maintain her composure in situations that would leave others shaken. Still, even she paused when she knelt beside the bodies.

The victims appeared to be teenagers, both with dark hair and slight builds. Their skin showed a pallor consistent with having been dead for at least a day, possibly longer, but it was the visible injuries that made Dr. Hoffman's expression grow grim.

Both bodies bore evidence of significant trauma. Strange circular marks ringed one victim's breasts—perfect rings of bruising that puzzled Dr. Hoffman. The patterns were unlike anything she had seen before, almost as if suction cups or some kind of vacuum device had been applied to create the distinctive marks. The other victim showed signs of violence focused on different areas of her body, with massive swelling and bruising that indicated prolonged, systematic abuse. Most disturbing, both victims displayed what appeared to be small puncture wounds—precise, deliberate injuries that spoke to prolonged suffering rather than a quick death.

The unusual nature of the injuries would later lead investigators to consult sex shop catalogs and examine vacuum-based devices used for body modification, trying to understand what kind of implement could have created such distinctive trauma. The circular marks became one of the most puzzling aspects of the crime scene, a detail that would haunt investigators as they tried to piece together exactly what had been done to the victims.

Dr. Hoffman told Detective Müller that the girls had been tortured; this wasn't a crime of passion or opportunity. Someone had taken their time. The careful positioning of the bodies, the remote location, the methodical nature of the injuries… Everything pointed to a killer who had planned this carefully and might well strike again.

———

The call to both families came on a Tuesday evening, October 11. Detective Müller had dreaded making it, knowing that the moment he spoke, he would be destroying the last fragile hope that Jasmin and Yvonne might still be alive somewhere.

The drive to the morgue in Gießen passed in a blur for both families. The identifications took only moments. Both families recognized their daughters immediately, despite the ashen hue of death and the clinical setting. Jasmin's mother collapsed into sobs that echoed off the tile walls, while Yvonne's father had to support his wife as her legs gave out beneath her.

Dr. Hoffman's preliminary examination revealed disturbing details that she shared only with the investigation team. Both girls showed signs of having been restrained for an extended period before their deaths. The circular marks on Yvonne's chest were consistent with tight bindings that had cut off circulation, creating distinctive bruising patterns. Jasmin's injuries suggested focused trauma to her genital area, indicating sexual violence of an extreme nature.

Most puzzling, however, were the small puncture wounds found on both bodies. They appeared to have been made with medical needles or similar sharp instruments, inflicted with surgical precision in areas designed to cause maximum pain without immediately causing death. The pattern suggested someone with either medical knowledge or a disturbing familiarity with human anatomy.

The cause of death was something Detective Müller hadn't expected: chloroform poisoning. Both girls had died from respiratory failure caused by an overdose of the volatile anesthetic. This discovery raised new questions about the killer's methods and knowledge. Chloroform wasn't something most people had access to or knew how to use effectively.

The bodies had been washed thoroughly before being dumped, removing most trace evidence that might have identified the perpetrator. But the killer had made one mistake: A single white cotton sock was found lying across Jasmin's body, apparently dropped during the positioning of the corpses.

As news of the murders spread through Limburg and the surrounding communities, fear settled over the region like a fog. Parents kept their teenage children home at night, and the local discotheques saw their attendance plummet. The killer was still out there, and nobody knew who might be next.

———

Detective Müller found himself leading the largest criminal investigation in the region's recent history. The brutal nature of the murders had captured public attention throughout Germany, with national media outlets picking up the story and putting pressure on local authorities to find the killer quickly.

The investigation team established a timeline of the girls' final hours with painstaking precision. Security cameras at both discotheques had captured images of Jasmin and Yvonne throughout the evening, showing them laughing and dancing. The last confirmed sighting placed them in the parking lot of Anyway at around 4:00 a.m., talking to someone near a dark-colored sedan.

Witness interviews provided frustratingly little additional information. The couple who had approached the girls seemed to have been deliberately forgettable—average in every way, careful not to draw attention to themselves.

The forensic evidence from the crime scene painted a picture of a methodical, organized killer. The remote location where the bodies were dumped was approximately fifty kilometers from the nightclub, suggesting someone familiar with the rural roads and forests of the region. The careful washing of the bodies and positioning of the corpses indicated someone who had thought through the process of disposing of evidence.

Most disturbing was the nature of the torture the girls had endured. Dr. Hoffman's full autopsy report revealed that both victims had been alive during their ordeal, suffering for hours before succumbing to the chloroform. The specific pattern of injuries suggested someone acting out detailed fantasies of sexual violence and control.

Weeks turned into months as the investigation continued. Police interviewed hundreds of potential witnesses and suspects, following up on every tip that came in through their hotline. They spoke to attendees from both nightclubs, tracked down everyone who had been seen in the vicinity that night, and conducted extensive background checks on anyone with a history of sexual violence.

But the killer seemed to have vanished as completely as if he had never existed. No new evidence surfaced, no witnesses came forward with useful information, and the forensic evidence from the crime scene yielded no immediate leads.

In June 1995, the case was featured on "Aktenzeichen XY… ungelöst" (Case File XY... Unsolved), Germany's most popular unsolved crimes television program. The broadcast included a detailed reconstruction of the girls' final hours and an appeal for information from the public. A reward of 25,000 Deutsche Marks was offered for information leading to the arrest of the killer.

The program generated hundreds of tips, but none provided the breakthrough investigators desperately needed. The killer remained at large, and the families of Jasmin and Yvonne were left to struggle with grief that had no resolution.

———

Three years had passed since the murders when the phone call came. Detective Müller, now leading other investigations but still haunted by the unsolved case, answered to find an anonymous caller on the line. The voice mentioned looking into a man named Lutz Kecke, offering no other explanation before the line went dead.

Lutz Kecke lived in the Westerwald region, about an hour's drive from both the nightclub and the forest where the bodies had been found. He worked as a bricklayer, had no significant criminal record, and appeared to live a quiet life with his wife in the small village of Girkenroth.

Detective Müller arranged for an interview with Kecke, approaching it as a routine follow-up rather than focusing on him as a suspect. Kecke appeared cooperative but unremarkable: a middle-aged man with graying hair and calloused hands who seemed genuinely puzzled about why police would want to speak with him.

The interview yielded nothing useful, and without additional evidence, the investigation into Kecke stalled. Criminal profilers had theorized that the killer likely lived closer to where the bodies had been dumped, making Kecke seem like an unlikely suspect anyway.

Years continued to pass. Detective Müller retired, handing the case files over to younger investigators who brought fresh eyes to the evidence but no new insights.

———

By 2000, DNA testing had evolved dramatically from the primitive techniques available when the murders first occurred. Professor Bernd Brinkmann, a renowned forensic specialist at the University of Münster, had developed new methods for extracting genetic material from trace evidence that had previously been considered too degraded to analyze.

The white sock found at the crime scene had been carefully preserved in the evidence room for six years. When Professor Brinkmann examined it using the latest techniques, he was able to extract DNA from sweat and skin cells that had been invisible to earlier testing methods.

The result was a clear male genetic profile. It was the first concrete lead the investigation had generated in years.

Armed with this breakthrough, investigators launched one of Germany's largest DNA mass screenings to date. They compiled a list of over 1,100 men who had been connected to the case in various ways: witnesses from the nightclub, individuals who had been interviewed during the initial investigation, and anyone whose name had come up in tips or leads over the years.

Lutz Kecke was among those summoned for voluntary DNA testing. The anonymous tip from 1997 had kept his name in the files, making him an obvious candidate for inclusion in the screening.

The testing began in the summer of 2001. Most men came willingly, understanding that their cooperation would help eliminate them as suspects and potentially solve a notorious crime that had terrified their communities.

Then, in September 2001, a match appeared. The DNA profile from sample number 847 was identical to the genetic material found on the sock. Sample 847 belonged to Lutz Kecke.

Seven years after Jasmin G. and Yvonne H. had disappeared from a nightclub parking lot, their killer finally had a name.

Lutz Kecke

September 18, 2001, started as an ordinary Tuesday for Lutz Kecke. He arrived at his construction job in Bilkheim just after 7:00 a.m., as he had done for years. At 10:30 a.m., several unmarked police cars pulled up to the construction site.

Detective Inspector Andreas Weber, who had taken over the case from the retired Müller, approached Kecke with backup officers flanking him. The construction site fell silent as workers stopped what they were doing to watch the unfolding drama.

Kecke's face went white as he was placed under arrest. His hands began to tremble so violently that he dropped the trowel he had been holding. For a moment, he seemed unable to speak or move. Then, to the surprise of everyone present, he began to cry.

———

The confession began almost immediately. During the drive to the police station, Kecke started talking and seemed unable to stop. Seven years of guilt and fear poured out of him in a rambling stream of admissions and explanations that both horrified and fascinated investigators.

Detective Weber pressed for details, and Kecke provided them with a clinical detachment that seemed disconnected from the enormity of what he was describing. He spoke about the planning, the approach at the nightclub, the chloroform, and the hours of torture that followed as if he were recounting a mundane work project rather than the brutal murder of two teenagers.

But there was something else in his confession that caught Weber's attention: Kecke's repeated use of the word "we."

When pressed about who else was involved, Kecke revealed that his wife, Monika, had been there and had helped. The revelation that the murders had been committed by a married couple sent shockwaves through the investigation team.

When police arrived at the Kecke home that evening to arrest Monika, they found her waiting calmly in the kitchen. It was as if she, too, had been expecting this moment. Unlike her husband, however, she did not confess immediately. She denied everything, claiming that Lutz had problems and made things up.

But the evidence was already mounting against her. Forensic tests on material collected from Yvonne's body had detected female DNA—genetic material that matched samples taken from Monika during her arrest. The scientific proof was irrefutable: She had been in direct contact with at least one of the victims.

Faced with this evidence, Monika's denials crumbled. Over the course of several interviews, the full scope of the crime emerged. It was a tale of sexual sadism, psychological manipulation, and a relationship so twisted that it had culminated in the torture and murder of two innocent girls.

———

The confession that emerged over the following weeks painted a picture of a relationship built on violence and sustained by shared secrets that grew progressively darker. Lutz Kecke's background revealed a troubled childhood marked by early separation from his mother and years spent in institutional care. Psychiatrists who examined him identified early trauma that had distorted his sexual development, creating what they diagnosed as an extreme form of sexual sadism.

Lutz's sexual practices had been escalating for years. Normal relations no longer satisfied him, and he had begun seeking increasingly violent encounters inspired by pornographic material depicting extreme sadomasochistic practices. Most of his partners had fled when they'd discovered his violent tendencies, but Monika had stayed.

A mother of three children from a previous marriage, Monika seemed willing to endure almost any abuse rather than face life alone. The interviews revealed years of systematic torture at her husband's hands—sessions where she was bound, beaten, and subjected to the same kinds of violence that Jasmin and Yvonne would later experience.

According to both their accounts, the night of October 8, 1994, had begun with an argument between the couple. Lutz had grown frustrated with the limitations of their usual routine, expressing fantasies about expanding their activities to include strangers. It was Monika who had suggested they find someone from the disco.

The plan they developed was methodical in its cruelty. Monika would approach potential victims, using her maternal appearance to gain their trust. Once the targets were isolated, Lutz would subdue them with chloroform for transport to their home in Girkenroth.

What happened next, in the bedroom of the Keckes' modest house, defied comprehension. Both suspects provided detailed accounts of the hours-long torture session that began in the early morning hours of October 9. They described how they carried the unconscious girls in sacks into their bedroom, where Lutz enacted his sadistic fantasies with methodical precision.

The torture was systematic and deliberate. Lutz focused much of his violence on the girls' chests and genitals, using ropes, medical needles, and sharp blades. Yvonne, who had larger breasts, had cords bound tightly around her chest repeatedly, causing the distinctive circular bruises that would later puzzle investigators. Lutz inflicted puncture wounds on her nipples using injection needles and cut her with sharp instruments. Jasmin suffered different but equally horrific abuse—while her breasts also showed injuries from binding and blunt force, the most severe trauma was inflicted on her genitals, causing massive swelling and bruising from violent assault.

Both girls were kept unconscious with repeated applications of chloroform whenever they began to stir, meaning the Keckes administered the dangerous anesthetic multiple times throughout the ordeal. The forensic evidence later confirmed that all injuries were inflicted while the victims were still alive, disproving any claims that the mutilation occurred after death. The torture had continued for hours, until the repeated chloroform doses finally caused fatal respiratory and cardiac failure.

The disposal of the bodies was planned with the same cold efficiency as the murders themselves. After the girls died, the Keckes meticulously washed the corpses to remove semen, blood, and any trace evidence that could identify them. They placed the clean bodies back into the sacks, and Lutz later described with chilling casualness how he had positioned one sack against a radiator and another against a wardrobe overnight before going to sleep.

The following evening, they transported the bodies in their car to the remote forest location near Hüttenberg-Volpertshausen, approximately fifty kilometers away. They deliberately arranged the crime scene to suggest the work of a lone sexual predator, hoping to misdirect the investigation away from a local married couple.

For seven years, they had lived with their secret. Lutz had continued his work as a bricklayer while Monika had tended to her children, both maintaining the facade of a normal marriage while harboring knowledge of their unspeakable crime.

As the investigation concluded and preparations for trial began, the small village of Girkenroth struggled to comprehend how such evil had existed in their midst for so long. Neighbors recalled the Keckes as quiet, unremarkable people who kept to themselves.

————

The trial of Lutz and Monika Kecke began in August 2002 at the Landgericht Limburg, nearly eight years after the crime. The case was prosecuted as a double murder with sexual motive, and both husband and wife were charged with acting in concert to abduct, torture, and kill the two girls.

During the proceedings, conflicting testimonies emerged as each defendant attempted to shift blame. Monika portrayed herself as a helpless victim of her husband's domination, claiming she had acted under his influence and was psychologically subjugated to him. She admitted to approaching and luring the girls into the car, but she maintained that Lutz was the mastermind and sole active killer.

Lutz, however, had recanted his initial confession and taken a different approach. In a written statement, he blamed Monika for everything, depicting her as the true sadist who enjoyed being tortured and had suggested they find victims to torture together. He claimed the deaths were accidental, asserting that both girls had already died from the chloroform when they unpacked them at home.

Forensic experts testified that the girls' injuries occurred while they were alive, contradicting Lutz's claims. The evidence firmly placed both defendants at the scene and in contact with the victims through DNA analysis.

On March 26, 2003, the Limburg court delivered its verdict. Monika Kecke was found fully guilty and sentenced to life in prison for two counts of murder. The court rejected her portrayal as a bystander, stating that without her contribution, the crime would have been inconceivable. Judge Karin Walter emphasized that, unlike her husband, Monika had no mental impairment and was fully accountable for her actions.

For Lutz Kecke, the court acknowledged psychiatric findings of extreme sexual deviation. They ruled that his capacity for guilt was partially diminished due to his severe paraphilic disorder. Instead of a mandatory life term for murder, Lutz received fifteen years' imprisonment followed by indefinite confinement in a secure psychiatric facility. In effect, this meant Lutz would not be released until deemed no longer dangerous, which could potentially be never.

The harsh difference in sentences reflected how the court weighed the defendants' mental states. Monika's active luring of the victims made her equally responsible, while Lutz's sadistic sexual deviation was considered a mitigating mental condition balanced by indefinite psychiatric commitment to protect society.

Today, more than two decades after the murders, Monika Kecke remains incarcerated, having served her minimum term but with little prospect of release given the horrific nature of her crimes. Lutz completed his prison sentence in 2018 but was transferred to a secure psychiatric facility as ordered, where he remains confined indefinitely.

The case stands as one of Germany's most disturbing examples of how ordinary-seeming people can harbor extraordinary evil, as well as how advances in forensic science can bring justice even when hope seems lost. For the families of Jasmin G. and Yvonne H., the convictions provided some measure of closure, though the pain of their loss continues to this day.

CHAPTER 6
THE WITCH'S CASTLE

The hunters thought it was a mannequin at first.

Donn and Ralph Foley had been walking through the harvested soybean field along Lemon Road that cold Saturday morning, January 11, 1992, when they spotted what looked like a burned department store dummy dumped in the frost-covered earth. The blackened form lay twisted and unrecognizable, steam still rising from the charred remains in the bitter Indiana air.

But mannequins don't have teeth—and this thing had a perfect set of them, gleaming white against the destruction.

At 10:55 a.m., the Jefferson County Sheriff's office received a call that would shatter the quiet community of Madison, Indiana.

———

Just hours before this grisly discovery, twelve-year-old Shanda Renée Sharer had been sleeping peacefully in her father's house in Jeffersonville, Indiana. To anyone who knew her, Shanda embodied pure energy and joy. Her mother, Jacque, described her as "bubbly" and "outgoing," with a tender heart that drew people to her like moths to a flame.

Shanda's world revolved around constant motion. She threw herself into cheerleading, volleyball, softball, and basketball with the same enthusiasm she brought to everything else in her young life. When she wasn't on a sports field, she could be found writing poetry or making new friends with an ease that adults envied.

The past six months had brought significant changes for the Sharer family. After her parents' divorce, Shanda had bounced between homes, spending weekdays with her mother in New Albany and weekends with her father, Stephen, in Jeffersonville. In fall 1991, she'd started seventh grade at Hazelwood Middle School in New Albany, where she'd quickly settled into the social rhythms of teenage life.

It was at Hazelwood that Shanda first encountered Amanda Heavrin, a fourteen-year-old with striking features and an air of confidence that commanded attention. Their meeting was hardly romantic. The two girls got into a physical altercation that landed them both in detention, but during those hours of forced proximity, something unexpected blossomed between them.

Amanda and Shanda began passing notes, their friendship deepening with each exchanged secret. The questions grew more personal: "I like girls, do you?" By October 1991, they were attending school dances together as dates, holding hands in hallways, and navigating the confusing waters of first love with all the intensity that only teenagers can muster.

But their happiness was being watched by jealous eyes.

———

Melinda Loveless had ruled her small corner of the teenage social world through intimidation and unpredictable rage. At sixteen, she carried herself with the swagger of someone who had learned early that fear was often more powerful than friendship. Her relationship with Amanda Heavrin in 1990 had been passionate and possessive, the kind of teenage romance that burned bright and left scars when it ended.

When Melinda spotted Amanda and Shanda together at a school dance in October 1991, something dark and primal awakened in her. She didn't just feel replaced—she felt erased. In front of dozens of classmates, Melinda confronted Shanda with words that would echo ominously in the weeks to come.

"I'm going to kill you," she said, her voice carrying the kind of cold certainty that made everyone around them step back.

Melinda Loveless

It wasn't just teenage drama. Students who witnessed the confrontation later described the look in Melinda's eyes as genuinely frightening. Amanda reportedly received death threat letters that she turned over to a youth prosecutor, but no meaningful action was taken. The adult world, it seemed, was content to dismiss teenage conflicts as harmless melodrama.

Shanda's parents weren't taking any chances. Concerned about the escalating threats, they pulled their daughter from Hazelwood Middle School and enrolled her at Our Lady of Perpetual Help School, a Catholic institution where they hoped she would be safer. Shanda joined the girls' basketball team and threw herself into her new environment with characteristic enthusiasm.

But transferring schools hadn't eliminated the problem; it had only given Melinda more time to nurture her hatred.

For weeks, Melinda had been showing other girls a knife, explaining her plans for Shanda with the casual tone someone might use to discuss weekend shopping plans. She found a willing accomplice in seventeen-year-old Laurie Tackett, a troubled girl who had dropped out of high school and claimed to hear voices commanding her to commit violence.

Laurie's fascination with the occult had deepened after her fifteenth birthday. She pretended to be possessed by someone she called "Deanna the Vampire" and told friends she believed it was her destiny to murder someone. Her mother would later testify to this chilling statement, describing how her daughter seemed to anticipate violence with an almost religious fervor.

The two older girls began recruiting others for their plan. Hope Rippey, fifteen, had been friends with Laurie for years and found herself drawn into conversations about "doing something" to Shanda. Fourteen-year-old Toni Lawrence, despite coming from the most stable background of the group, had her own reasons for feeling disconnected from the world around her.

As 1991 drew to a close, Melinda's planning intensified. She wasn't just talking about hurting Shanda anymore—she was methodically working out the details of how to kill her.

———

January 10, 1992, started like any other Friday evening. Laurie Tackett picked up Hope and Toni from Madison, telling them they were going to kill Shanda Sharer. The casual way she delivered this information, as if announcing a trip to the mall, would haunt both younger girls for the rest of their lives.

They drove to New Albany to collect Melinda, then headed to a punk rock show in Louisville. For a few hours, they were just teenagers at a concert, lost in the music and energy of the crowd. But as midnight approached, the real purpose of their evening began to take shape.

Just after 12:00 a.m. on January 11, they drove to Jeffersonville, Indiana, where Shanda was spending the weekend with her father. The house sat quietly in the darkness, its occupants asleep and unaware of the evil gathering outside their door.

Hope and Toni approached the front door while Melinda hid in the back seat under a blanket, gripping a knife with white knuckles. When Shanda answered their knock, the girls put on their most innocent faces.

"Amanda wants to see you at the Witch's Castle," Hope said.

The Witch's Castle was a local landmark near Mistletoe Falls, an abandoned stone building deep in the woods where teenagers often gathered. Shanda, appearing at the door in her nightgown, was excited at the prospect of seeing Amanda. The mention of her girlfriend's name was all the motivation Shanda needed.

She quickly dressed and followed the girls to their car, chattering excitedly about Amanda as she settled into the back seat. The moment the door closed, Melinda emerged from under the blanket like a predator striking its prey.

The knife pressed against Shanda's throat, and the cheerful twelve-year-old who had bounded out of her father's house transformed instantly into a terrified child begging for her life.

"Please don't hurt me," Shanda whispered. "I'll do whatever you want."

But mercy was not part of Melinda's plan.

———

They drove first to the Witch's Castle, where bare winter trees cast twisted shadows in the moonlight. In this isolated spot, they forced Shanda to strip and tied her up with rope, the frozen ground cutting into her bare skin as they debated what to do next.

Shanda's pleas for mercy grew more desperate. She promised to leave Amanda alone, to transfer schools, to disappear completely if they would just let her go home. But her words fell on deaf ears. Melinda and Laurie seemed energized by her terror, feeding off her fear like vampires drawing strength from blood.

They loaded her back into the car and drove to an abandoned building, where the torture escalated. Laurie produced a tire iron and began beating Shanda while Melinda held her down. The younger girl's screams echoed through the empty structure, but no one was around to hear them.

Next, they drove to Laurie's house, where her parents slept upstairs, unaware that their daughter was committing unspeakable acts in their basement. Here, prosecutors would later allege that sexual assault began, with both girls taking turns violating Shanda with the tire iron while she begged them to stop.

Hours passed in a blur of violence and degradation. Shanda's initial defiance had long since crumbled into whimpering surrender. She called for her mother between gasps of pain, her voice growing weaker as the night wore on.

As dawn approached, the girls made a chilling decision. They weren't just going to kill Shanda—they were going to burn her alive.

They stopped at a gas station, where Hope filled a two-liter Pepsi bottle with gasoline while Laurie kept Shanda subdued in the car. The station attendant would later tell police that the teenage customers seemed completely normal—a haunting reminder of how ordinary evil can appear.

———

The field along Lemon Road stretched on, empty and desolate in the early morning light. Frost covered the stubble of last year's soybean crop, and the air was sharp enough to turn breath to vapor. It was here that four teenage girls dragged their broken victim from the car and prepared to commit their final act of brutality.

Shanda could barely walk. The hours of torture had left her beaten, bloodied, and barely conscious. Through swollen lips, she made one last plea to the humanity she hoped still existed in her captors.

"Mommy," she whispered through a mouth filled with blood.

Hope Rippey stood with the gasoline container, her hands shaking. Even now, after hours of participating in this nightmare, she hesitated. For a moment, it seemed like someone might finally say stop.

Instead, the other girls screamed at her to hurry up.

Hope poured the gasoline over Shanda's battered body. Melinda struck the match.

The flames erupted instantly, consuming the twelve-year-old girl who had been writing poetry and playing basketball just hours before. Shanda's final screams cut through the morning air before fading into silence.

The four girls stood watching their victim burn, then calmly got back in their car and drove away.

———

At 9:30 a.m., the four teenagers walked into a McDonald's restaurant and ordered breakfast. They sat in a booth, laughing and comparing their sausage patties to Shanda's burned body. Other customers later described the girls as seeming "normal" and "happy." Just typical teenagers starting their Saturday morning.

But the weight of what they had done was already beginning to fracture their group. Toni Lawrence, who had participated least in the actual violence, found herself unable to maintain the pretense that everything was normal. As the day wore on, guilt and horror overwhelmed her.

That evening, at 8:20 p.m., Toni Lawrence walked into the Jefferson County Sheriff's office with her parents by her side. She asked to speak with Detective Stephen Thomas Henry, and she proceeded to confess to one of the most brutal murders in Indiana history.

Her detailed account provided investigators with a complete timeline of the eight-hour torture session. Hope Rippey soon followed with her own statement, and within hours, police had more than enough evidence to begin making arrests.

In one of the most disturbing revelations, investigators learned that Melinda and Laurie had actually shown Amanda Heavrin the bloody evidence in their car trunk the day after the murder. Amanda was reportedly shocked to realize they had been telling the truth about killing Shanda, but she chose not to contact the police. It was a decision that would later draw harsh public criticism.

————

Detective Henry had worked hundreds of cases during his career, but nothing had prepared him for Toni Lawrence's confession. As the fifteen-year-old girl described hour after hour of torture, Henry found himself struggling to maintain his professional composure.

The next morning, police descended on the crime scene along Lemon Road. The hunters' discovery took on new meaning as investigators realized they were looking at the remains of a child who had suffered unimaginable agony before her death.

Dr. George Nichols, Kentucky's Chief Medical Examiner, assisted Indiana authorities in conducting the autopsy that confirmed investigators' worst fears. Shanda had been alive when the fire had consumed her. The cause of death was burns and smoke inhalation, but the examination revealed the full scope of her torture: ligature marks from being tied up, multiple stab wounds, severe beating injuries, and evidence of brutal sexual assault.

Physical evidence began mounting against the perpetrators. Shanda's bloody handprints were found in the trunk of Laurie's car, along with her socks. Dental records confirmed the victim's identity, though her mother would later say she didn't need scientific proof—she knew her daughter was gone the moment police had knocked on her door.

The arrests came swiftly. Melinda Loveless showed no emotion when police took her into custody. Laurie Tackett seemed almost relieved, as if the voices in her head had finally been satisfied. Hope Rippey broke down crying, while Toni Lawrence maintained the cooperative attitude that had led her to confess in the first place.

———

Madison, Indiana, was a town where people left their doors unlocked and children played outside until dark. The murder of Shanda Sharer shattered that innocence in ways that residents would struggle to understand for years to come.

Sheriff Richard "Buck" Shipley, who had worked in law enforcement for decades, told reporters that it was the most horrific crime he had ever encountered. The idea that four teenage girls could commit such calculated brutality challenged everything the community thought it knew about their children.

Local churches held special services. School counselors worked overtime trying to help students process the unthinkable. Parents found themselves having conversations with their teenagers that they never imagined they would need to have.

But nowhere was the devastation more complete than in the Sharer family home.

———

Jacque Vaught received the phone call every parent dreads at 4:00 a.m. on January 12. Police officers were at her door, asking her to come to the station. They wouldn't tell her why over the phone, but their tone conveyed everything she needed to know.

"She was a baby," Jacque would later say. "She was my child. She was 12 years old, and that's how I'll always be able to remember her."

The aftermath would destroy Shanda's father as surely as fire had destroyed his daughter. Stephen Sharer began drinking heavily, consumed by guilt over his failure to protect Shanda. According to Jacque, he "did everything he could to kill himself besides put a gun to his head." He died of alcoholism in 2005 at age fifty-three, another victim of that terrible night in January 1992.

Driven by grief, Jacque left her career to advocate for other victims' families, establishing the Shanda Sharer Scholarship Fund. She appeared on television shows and spoke at conferences, determined that her daughter's death would not be meaningless.

————

The trials of the four teenagers captured national attention, raising difficult questions about how society should handle juveniles who commit adult crimes. Despite their ages, ranging from fourteen to seventeen, all four were tried as adults.

The evidence was overwhelming. Toni Lawrence's confession, Hope Rippey's corroborating statements, and the physical evidence left no doubt about what had happened during those eight hours of terror. The only question was what price the perpetrators would pay.

The sentences reflected both the severity of the crime and the ages of the defendants. Toni Lawrence, who had cooperated fully with police and shown genuine remorse, received twenty years. Hope Rippey got thirty-five years after an initial sentence of sixty was reduced. Laurie Tackett and Melinda Loveless each received sixty years in prison.

During the sentencing hearings, more details about the perpetrators' backgrounds emerged. Melinda's history of severe sexual abuse at the hands of her father painted a picture of a child who had never known safety or normalcy. Laurie's documented mental illness and hallucinations suggested a young woman who had been failed by every system designed to help her.

However, the judge was unmoved by these explanations, saying the gruesome nature of the crime—involving planning and resulting in the confinement of the victim for a period of over eight hours—demanded significant punishment regardless of the defendants' ages or backgrounds.

———

Over the years that followed, the four women would take dramatically different paths. Toni Lawrence, released after serving nine years, disappeared from public view and rebuilt her life in anonymity. Hope Rippey served fourteen years before her release in 2006, maintaining a low profile and working to make amends for her role in the crime.

Laurie Tackett served twenty-six years, during which time she earned her GED and college degrees, participated in extensive therapy, and gradually gained control over the mental illness that had contributed to her violence. She was released on January 11, 2018, exactly twenty-six years after the murder.

Melinda Loveless served the longest sentence, spending more than twenty-six years behind bars before her release in September 2019. During her incarceration, she underwent intensive therapy to address her childhood trauma and the rage that had consumed her teenage years. In a development that shocked many observers, she eventually developed a correspondence with Jacque Vaught, Shanda's mother.

In one of the most remarkable acts of forgiveness in criminal justice history, Jacque donated a puppy named "Angel" to Melinda Loveless for service dog training. The gesture stunned everyone who knew the case, but Jacque explained that holding onto hatred was destroying her as surely as it had destroyed her ex-husband.

The relationship between the victim's mother and the perpetrator became one of the most extraordinary aspects of the case's aftermath. Melinda later expressed deep gratitude to Jacque for the gesture, saying that it had helped her heal and grow.

———

Today, more than thirty years after that terrible night in January 1992, the Shanda Sharer case continues to reverberate through discussions of juvenile justice, childhood trauma, and the capacity for both evil and redemption in human nature.

The four teenage girls who committed this crime have all been released from prison, having served their sentences and supposedly paid their debt to society. They are now middle-aged women, some with children of their own, trying to build lives in the shadow of the worst thing they will ever do.

But Shanda Sharer remains forever twelve years old, frozen in time at the moment when hatred and jealousy extinguished a light that should have burned for decades to come. Her poetry will never be finished. Her athletic potential will never be realized. The friendships she might have formed and the love she might have given to the world died with her in that frozen field.

The hunters who found her body on that cold January morning could never have imagined the story behind the burned remains they discovered. They saw the end result of eight hours of torture that began with teenage jealousy and ended with calculated murder. They witnessed the final chapter of a story that started with a schoolgirl crush and concluded with one of the most brutal crimes in American history.

In the end, four young women destroyed their own lives in their determination to destroy another. They succeeded in killing Shanda Sharer, but they also killed the children they had been and any chance they might have had for normal, happy lives. Their crime created multiple victims—not just Shanda, but her family, their own families, and a community that lost its innocence on a winter morning when evil revealed itself in the most unexpected form.

CHAPTER 7

VOICES AND VIOLENCE

The house at the corner of Higbee Avenue and 17th Street in Idaho Falls served as a sober living home for individuals navigating mental illness and recovery. The residents came and went, each carrying their own burdens and hopes for stability.

Hermann Hans Woerrlein had only been living there for a few months when March 2020 arrived. At fifty-one, the German-born man possessed an intellect that impressed those around him. "Extremely smart, super sweet, and a very nice guy," was how people described him. He spoke with the careful precision of someone for whom English was a second language, though his grasp of it was excellent. Hans, as most called him, had been traveling across the United States before settling temporarily in Idaho Falls. He still owned property back in Germany, and he spoke often of his desire to return home someday.

Hans struggled with his own demons—diagnosed schizophrenia and paranoia had brought him to this transitional housing. However, those who knew him found him engaging and personable. He was someone who could hold fascinating conversations about philosophy, religion, and the mysteries of existence. In the group home, such discussions were common currency among residents who often found solace in exploring life's deeper questions.

Douglass Taylor had arrived at the house around the same time. At thirty-two, he was nearly two decades younger than Hans, but his weathered appearance suggested a life that had aged him beyond his years. Where Hans was warm and talkative, Taylor kept more to himself, though he participated in the house's frequent discussions about religion and secret societies. The two men were assigned as roommates, a pairing that seemed unremarkable at the time.

Taylor's journey to this Idaho Falls group home had been long and troubled. Born in Burley, Idaho, his childhood had shown promise. He had excelled in mathematics and music, playing piano, guitar, and violin with natural ability. He'd even composed his own pieces. In track and field, he had demonstrated the same excellence that marked his academic pursuits.

But darkness had touched the Taylor family early. When Douglass was six, his father's employment took them to Utah. When he was eleven, they returned to Idaho due to another job change. His father's behavior became increasingly erratic—symptoms that resembled bipolar disorder, though no formal diagnosis was ever made. By the time Douglass was twelve, his parents had separated, his mother obtaining a protective order out of fear for their safety.

The devastating blow came when Douglass was fourteen. His father committed suicide, leaving behind a son who would never fully recover from the trauma. Depression settled over the teenage boy like a suffocating blanket, and medication became part of his daily routine for the first time.

Douglass Taylor graduated from high school in 2006 and tried to build a normal life. But at twenty, while working out of state, his world began to fracture in ways that medication couldn't fix. The voices started quietly at first, then grew louder and more insistent. Reality began to shift and bend around him in terrifying ways. The diagnosis, when it came, carried a weight that would define the rest of his life: schizophrenia.

His first mental health commitment in Minidoka County marked the beginning of a pattern that would repeat dozens of times over the next fourteen years. Hospitalization, treatment, brief stability, and then the inevitable slide back into chaos. By age twenty-one, his condition had progressed to schizoaffective disorder—a cruel combination of schizophrenia and bipolar disorder that made his mental landscape even more treacherous to navigate.

The worst episode came in 2009, when Douglass, gripped by religious delusions, fled to Canada seeking asylum. For months, his family had no idea where he was or if he was alive. When Canadian authorities finally released him and he returned home, his mother made the difficult decision to petition for legal guardianship. The court granted her request, recognizing that her son could no longer safely manage his own affairs.

For six years, she tried to provide the stability he needed. But in 2015, Douglass requested that she relinquish guardianship. Despite concerns from both the court and his mother about his instability and potential danger, the request was granted. He was twenty-seven years old and legally free to make his own decisions—decisions that too often involved discontinuing the medications that kept his symptoms at bay.

The cycle continued relentlessly. Between 2015 and early 2020, Douglass was hospitalized or civilly committed between twenty-nine and thirty-two times. Each stay followed the same pattern: crisis, commitment, treatment, brief stabilization, release, medication non-compliance, and another crisis. It was a revolving door that exhausted families, strained resources, and left Douglass perpetually on the edge of disaster.

The most recent commitment had occurred in November 2019, when Ada County placed him in State Hospital South in Blackfoot. He spent five weeks there, entering the treatment floor on December 16. But by January 21, 2020, just two days before his scheduled release, staff notes painted a troubling picture. Douglass was exhibiting bizarre behavior, refusing to comply with medication measurements, isolating himself from others, and showing minimal engagement in positive activities.

Despite these red flags, he was released on January 23, 2020. The hospital's decision reflected a harsh reality of the mental health system. Limited bed space meant that patients were often discharged as soon as they met minimal criteria for release, regardless of whether they were truly ready to function independently. Douglass was sent to a halfway house that offered little more than a roof over his head. There was no ongoing treatment, no real monitoring, and no safety net to catch him if he fell.

Seven weeks later, he was assigned a room in the Higbee Avenue group home, where he would meet Hermann Hans Woerrlein.

On the surface, the two men seemed to get along well enough. They shared meals, participated in house discussions, and navigated the routine of communal living without significant conflict. Hans continued to speak hopefully about returning to Germany, while Douglass struggled with the demons that had haunted him for over a decade. Neither man had any way of knowing that their paths would intersect in the most tragic way possible.

———

March 10, 2020, began like any other day at the group home. The routines were familiar: meals at regular times, medication schedules for those who maintained them, and the comfortable rhythm of people learning to rebuild their lives. Hans had spent part of the day engaged in one of his philosophical discussions with other residents—conversations that ranged from religion to mythology to the hidden forces that shaped human history.

Aaron, another resident, had been looking forward to an early bedtime. His room was in the basement, away from the main living areas upstairs. As he prepared for sleep at around 10:30 p.m., the house was settling into its usual quiet evening routine.

The first sound that penetrated his consciousness was muffled but urgent. Aaron paused in his bedtime preparations, straining to identify what he'd heard. Then it came again, clearer this time and unmistakably human: a voice calling out from somewhere upstairs.

"No, please stop!"

The words sent a chill through Aaron. The tone carried a desperation that cut through the normal sounds of the house like a blade. Someone was in trouble. Serious trouble.

Aaron didn't hesitate. He bolted from his basement room and took the stairs two at a time, his heart hammering as he raced toward whatever emergency awaited. The house seemed too quiet now, as if holding its breath.

He reached the main floor and followed the sound toward the kitchen. What he saw when he rounded the corner would haunt him for the rest of his life.

Hermann Hans Woerrlein lay on the kitchen floor in a spreading pool of blood. Standing over him was Douglass Taylor, holding a knife with a red handle. As Aaron watched in frozen horror, Taylor was pulling the blade from Hans's neck, the metal emerging slick and dark.

Douglass Taylor

For a moment that seemed to stretch into eternity, the three men were frozen in a scene of violence and shock. Then Taylor spotted Aaron in the doorway. Without a word, he dropped the knife and ran.

Aaron heard Taylor's footsteps pounding through the house, the front door slamming, and then silence except for the terrible sound of Hans's labored breathing. Blood continued to pool beneath the fallen man, and Aaron could see wounds across his body that spoke to the savagery of the attack.

Every instinct screamed at Aaron to help, but fear paralyzed him. Hans looked "too far gone," and a darker thought crept into Aaron's mind: If he tried to help and Hans died anyway, would the police think he was involved? Would they believe his story about walking in on the attack?

Instead of rendering aid, Aaron grabbed his phone and dialed 911.

———

An officer who happened to be nearby arrived at the Higbee Avenue address within minutes, finding Aaron waiting outside in a state of visible distress. The young man's words tumbled out in a rush: Taylor had stabbed Hans, there was blood everywhere, and Taylor had run away.

The officer called for backup and ambulance services before entering the house. In the kitchen, he found Hermann Hans Woerrlein motionless on the floor, surrounded by blood. The red-handled knife lay abandoned in the living room where Taylor had dropped it during his escape.

Paramedics arrived and worked frantically to stabilize Hans, but his injuries were catastrophic. They rushed him to

Eastern Idaho Regional Medical Center, though the outcome seemed grimly inevitable. Behind the blood-soaked scene they left behind, police began the methodical work of processing evidence and hunting for the suspect.

Other patrol units combed the area around the group home. They checked alleyways, abandoned buildings, and any place a man covered in blood might try to conceal himself. The search had been underway for less than ten minutes when an officer spotted a figure behind the Albertsons grocery store on 17th Street.

Douglass Taylor sat motionless in the shadows, his clothes soaked with blood. He made no attempt to run when officers approached, no effort to resist as they placed him in hand-cuffs. The blood covering his shirt and hands was still wet, the metallic smell unmistakable.

"Are you injured?" one officer asked, examining Taylor for wounds that might explain the blood.

Taylor shook his head. The blood wasn't his.

At 10:36 p.m., just minutes after the initial 911 call, Douglass Taylor was in custody. The hunt was over almost before it had begun, but the real mystery was just starting to unfold.

———

At the Bonneville County Law Enforcement Building, Detective Howard Schwicht prepared to interview the blood-covered suspect. Taylor had been read his rights and agreed to speak without an attorney present—a decision that played a significant role in understanding what had happened in that Idaho Falls kitchen.

"I'm responsible for the killing of Hermann Hans Woerrlein," Taylor said without preamble.

Detective Schwicht had handled countless interviews, but the matter-of-fact tone in Taylor's voice was unsettling. There was no emotion, no apparent remorse or shock. Taylor spoke as if discussing the weather.

"Can you tell me what happened?"

"I brutally stabbed that guy and made sure he was dead. I stabbed him about fifteen times and then slit his throat."

The detective made careful notes, but his questions about motive received answers that made no sense. Taylor claimed that Hans had been "trying to start a new cult with German mythology." He referred to the fifty-one-year-old victim as "young retard Hitler" and told detectives, "If someone is trying to start a large worldwide cult, I will eliminate that person. There are enough religions on this planet."

"What evidence did you have that he was starting a cult?" Detective Schwicht asked.

Taylor's explanations were rambling and incoherent. He spoke of conversations about religion and secret societies, discussions that other residents confirmed were common in the group home. But Taylor had interpreted these philosophical musings as something sinister—evidence of a nascent Nazi organization that he needed to stop.

As the interview continued, a disturbing picture emerged. This wasn't a crime of passion or sudden rage. Taylor admitted that he had "bought a knife intending to use it on someone in a lethal manner." He had planned the attack, chosen his method, and executed it with cold precision.

"I had been having thoughts of killing people for several years," he told the detective. "The day of my crime, I planned my method."

Detective Schwicht cross-referenced Taylor's claims with the evidence. Other residents were interviewed about Hans's behavior and conversations. Police searched for any indication that Hermann Hans Woerrlein had extremist beliefs or was involved in cult activity.

They found nothing. No Nazi propaganda, no evidence of recruitment, no suggestion that Hans was anything other than what he appeared to be: a mentally ill man trying to rebuild his life while engaging in the kind of philosophical discussions common among people searching for meaning in their struggles.

———

Meanwhile, at Eastern Idaho Regional Medical Center, doctors were fighting a losing battle. Hans's injuries were simply too severe. He had suffered seventeen stab wounds across his body, concentrated on his torso and left arm, but it was the six deep slashes across his neck that proved fatal. Taylor had nearly severed Hans's throat completely, causing massive blood loss and destroying vital structures.

Hermann Hans Woerrlein was pronounced dead shortly after arrival. A man who had survived mental illness, dislocation, and the challenges of building a new life in a foreign country had been murdered by his roommate over a delusion that existed only in the killer's fractured mind.

———

As news of the murder spread, questions began emerging about how Douglass Taylor had been free to commit such a violent act. His history painted a clear picture of a man in crisis, cycling through the mental health system without ever receiving the long-term stability he needed.

The most troubling revelation centered on his recent stay at State Hospital South. Just seven weeks before the murder, Taylor had been released despite staff observations of bizarre behavior and non-compliance with treatment. Notes from January 21, just two days before his discharge, documented his refusal to cooperate with medication protocols, his self-isolation, and his minimal engagement with therapeutic activities.

Yet hospital administrators, facing pressure to free up beds for new patients, had discharged him to a halfway house with no ongoing treatment or monitoring. The decision reflected a broader crisis in Idaho's mental health infrastructure—a system stretched so thin that patients were often released based on legal criteria rather than clinical readiness.

Taylor's mother had written letter after letter to courts and hospitals, begging them to recognize that her son needed long-term care. She had detailed his pattern of medication non-compliance and the danger he posed to himself and others when his symptoms went untreated. However, the system's hands were often tied by laws that prioritized patient freedom over public safety.

The tragedy might have been prevented if Taylor had been held longer, if better outpatient monitoring had been available, or if the group home had been equipped to recognize and respond to warning signs. Instead, a man with a fourteen-year history of violent ideation had been placed in close quarters with vulnerable individuals, with no safety net to prevent disaster.

———

By March 11, 2020, Douglass Taylor had been formally charged with first-degree murder. His bond was set at $500,000, an amount that ensured he would remain in custody while the legal system grappled with his case.

The competency evaluation was immediate and thorough. Despite his mental illness, Taylor was found capable of understanding the charges against him and assisting in his own defense. This determination meant the case could proceed, but it also raised questions about the relationship between mental illness and criminal responsibility.

For nearly two years, the case wound through the court system. The evidence was overwhelming—Taylor's confession, the physical evidence, the eyewitness testimony. Still, his attorneys faced the challenge of representing a client whose actions were clearly influenced by severe mental illness, even as the law held him responsible for those actions.

The preliminary hearing in January 2021 established that probable cause existed for the first-degree murder charge. Magistrate Judge Kent Gauchay ruled that Taylor had acted "with malice and forethought" and that the murder was "willful, deliberate, and premeditated." The case would proceed to district court, where the full weight of Idaho's criminal justice system would be brought to bear.

Initially, Taylor pleaded not guilty, setting the stage for a trial that would examine the intersection of mental illness and violent crime. As the evidence mounted and the reality of his situation became clear, however, plea negotiations began in earnest.

———

On December 15, 2021, Douglass Taylor appeared before District Judge Bruce L. Pickett and changed his plea to guilty. The decision spared Hermann Hans Woerrlein's family the trauma of a trial and eliminated any possibility that Taylor might escape conviction on a technicality.

The plea agreement also reflected the prosecution's confidence in their case while acknowledging the mitigating factor of Taylor's mental illness. Prosecutors agreed to recommend no more than twenty-five years to life, while the defense would argue for no more than fifteen years to life. This range ensured that Taylor would face significant punishment while leaving room for the court to consider his psychiatric history.

But even as Taylor accepted responsibility for his actions, disturbing details continued to emerge. According to Detective Schwicht's later testimony, in October 2021, he received a handwritten letter from Taylor attempting to recant his confession. In the letter, Taylor claimed that Aaron, the roommate who had called 911, was actually the killer. He alleged that his own confession had been false, the product of trauma and confusion.

Detective Schwicht investigated these new claims thoroughly, interviewing Aaron again and reviewing all the evidence. However, the allegations were baseless—they were a desperate attempt by Taylor to escape responsibility for his actions. Aaron was completely innocent, and Taylor's letter served only to demonstrate his continued disconnection from reality.

———

The sentencing hearing on February 9, 2022, brought together all the threads of this tragic story. Judge Pickett's courtroom was filled with the weight of competing narratives: mental illness versus personal responsibility, systemic failure versus individual accountability, mercy versus justice.

Public Defender Jason Gustaves painted a picture of a man failed by every institution meant to help him. He recounted Taylor's twenty-nine to thirty-two hospitalizations, his diagnosis with schizoaffective disorder, and the system's repeated failure to provide adequate long-term care. Idaho's mental health infrastructure, Gustaves argued, was "deeply flawed," creating a revolving door that inevitably led to tragedy.

"Hans didn't deserve to die," Gustaves acknowledged. "Two families didn't need to lose their families like this."

But Bonneville County Chief Deputy Prosecutor Alex Muir focused on the brutal reality of the crime itself. Seventeen stab wounds and six slashes to the throat. A victim who had begged for his life. A killer who had planned his method and purchased his weapon with lethal intent.

"This was extremely egregious, personal and violent and heinous," Muir argued. Mental illness might have explained Taylor's actions, but it didn't excuse them.

Prosecutors had chosen not to seek the death penalty, citing Taylor's documented mental illness as a mitigating factor. As prosecutor Muir noted, the victim's family had shown "more mercy to this defendant than the defendant showed to Hermann Woerrlein." They wanted justice for a man who had been trying to rebuild his life when it was cut short by senseless violence.

Judge Pickett listened to both sides before delivering his decision. He acknowledged the "horrifically sad" nature of Taylor's mental health struggles while emphasizing the "heinous nature of the crime and the premeditation that went into it."

"You chose not to check yourself into the hospital," the judge told Taylor. "Instead, you chose to purchase a knife. You chose to kill someone, and that someone happened to be your roommate."

The sentence reflected this balance: a unified life term with a minimum of twenty-seven years before parole eligibility. It was two years more than even the prosecution had requested, a signal that the court prioritized public safety and appropriate punishment over sympathy for the defendant's condition.

Taylor was also ordered to pay $5,000 in fines and $3,155 in restitution for Hans's funeral costs. When given the opportunity to speak, he declined to make any statement.

———

Taylor's appeal of his sentence was unsuccessful. In February 2023, the Idaho Court of Appeals upheld the conviction and sentence, finding that the district court had not abused its discretion. Douglass Taylor, now thirty-seven years old, remains incarcerated at the Idaho State Correctional Institution. His earliest possible parole date is March 11, 2047, when he will be fifty-nine years old.

Hermann Hans Woerrlein lies buried far from the German home he had hoped to see again. His death became a statistic in discussions about mental health policy and violence prevention, but for those who knew him, he remained a real person whose life had value beyond its tragic end.

The group home on Higbee Avenue continued to house vulnerable individuals seeking stability and recovery. Aaron, the witness whose quick thinking had led to Taylor's capture, struggled with the trauma of what he had seen. The residents who remained tried to rebuild their sense of safety in a place that had been forever changed by violence.

For Taylor's family, the tragedy represented the culmination of years of desperate attempts to get their loved one the help he needed. His mother and sister blamed not Douglass himself, but a system that had failed to provide adequate care for someone who clearly posed a danger to himself and others.

The case highlighted uncomfortable truths about the intersection of mental illness and violence. While the vast majority of people with mental health conditions are not violent, Taylor's story demonstrated what could happen when severe psychiatric illness went untreated in someone with a history of violent ideation. The warning signs had been there for years, documented in hospital records and court files, but the system's response had been inadequate to prevent tragedy.

In the end, two lives were destroyed that night in March 2020. Hermann Hans Woerrlein lost his life to senseless violence, and Douglass Taylor lost his freedom to the consequences of his actions. Behind them stood families shattered by loss and a community grappling with questions that had no easy answers.

The red-handled knife that ended Hans's life became evidence in a storage room, but the deeper wounds left by this crime—to families, to the community, and to faith in systems meant to protect the vulnerable—would take much longer to heal. Some might never heal at all.

CHAPTER 8

THE FORBIDDEN CLOSET

E lizabeth Kalina's hands trembled as she dialed 911 at 5:00 a.m. on that July morning in 2010. The nineteen-year-old stared at the insulated cooler she'd discovered in the forbidden closet, her voice barely steady as she spoke to the dispatcher.

"I think I found human remains in my mother's closet."

The operator's questions came rapid-fire. Where exactly had she found them? How long had they been there? Was anyone else in the apartment?

Elizabeth couldn't answer most of the questions. All she knew was that her mother had always kept this particular closet locked, warning her daughter never to go inside. For years, Michele Kalina had maintained an iron rule about that storage space in their high-rise apartment on Court Street in Reading, Pennsylvania. The building housed mostly seniors and disabled residents.

But curiosity had finally won over obedience, and what Elizabeth had found defied every explanation she could imagine.

―――――

Within minutes, patrol officers arrived at the apartment building. The morning was already warm, promising another sweltering July day in southeastern Pennsylvania. The officers examined the skeletal remains Elizabeth had discovered in a cooler, turning the bones over in their hands with casual indifference. After a brief consultation in the hallway, they delivered their verdict with the confidence of men who had seen everything: The bones weren't human. Probably animal bones from someone's hunting trips. The family could dispose of them in the regular trash.

Elizabeth watched the police leave, but something gnawed at her stomach like a persistent ache. The bones hadn't looked like anything from a deer or rabbit she'd ever seen. They appeared too small, too delicate—and there were more containers in that closet. Containers her mother had specifically forbidden anyone from touching for as long as Elizabeth could remember.

The nineteen-year-old spent the morning pacing the apartment, unable to shake her unease. Her father, Jeffrey— disabled and confined to managing their household while Michele worked—tried to reassure her that the police knew what they were talking about. However, Elizabeth's instincts screamed that something was terribly wrong.

Hours later, driven by a compulsion she couldn't explain, Elizabeth and Jeffrey made a second discovery that would change their lives forever. Deep in the recesses of the forbidden closet, they found more containers: a storage container, a plastic tub, and a cardboard box. One container was filled to the brim with a massive concrete block that appeared deliberately constructed and felt impossibly heavy for its size. The weight suggested something substantial had been embedded within the cement.

This time, when they called the police, Elizabeth's voice carried more urgency. The responding officers arrived with a far more serious demeanor than their morning colleagues. They examined the cement block with growing concern, noting its suspicious weight. Unlike the earlier team, these officers recognized they were potentially dealing with something much more sinister.

What they couldn't know was that the first set of bones—the ones their fellow officers had dismissed as animal remains— were already in a garbage truck heading toward the Conestoga Landfill in New Morgan, Berks County. The family, trusting the initial police assessment, had thrown them away just hours earlier.

———

Chief County Detective Michael Gombar had been handling cases for Berks County since 2008, dealing with everything from domestic disputes to drug trafficking. However, when he arrived at the Court Street apartment building and saw what forensic specialists had confirmed, he knew immediately this case would be unlike anything he'd encountered.

The remains were unmistakably human. Not just human— infant remains, stored for years in carefully sealed containers with methods that suggested meticulous planning.

The apartment belonged to Michele Kalina, a forty-four- year-old home health aide who worked for a regional health- care agency. According to her employment records, Michele had maintained an exemplary fourteen-year work record, often working seventy-hour weeks without complaint. Her supervisors consistently rated her performance as exceptional.

But Michele wasn't at the apartment when investigators arrived. When Jeffrey had told her about the police visits, her reaction had been immediate and telling. She had grabbed her purse and fled the building, telling Jeffrey, "I don't know where to go. I can't find peace there."

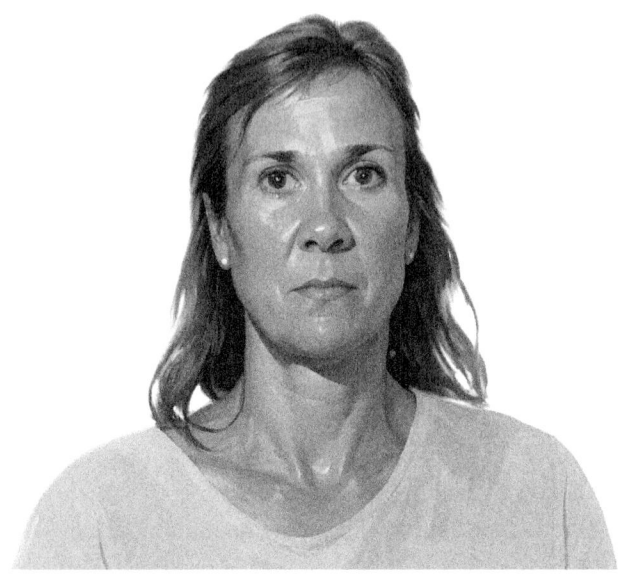

Michele Kalina

Her attempt to flee would later be cited as evidence of consciousness of guilt.

Using X-ray technology to examine the containers without disturbing potential evidence, investigators made an even more chilling discovery on August 11. The cement block contained the skeletal remains of an infant deliberately encased in concrete. Someone had taken considerable time and effort to permanently entomb the tiny body.

"We conducted an X-ray, and it revealed there was an unknown mass in the cement block," Gombar told reporters.

The investigators now faced the disturbing reality that they were dealing with multiple infant deaths concealed over an unknown period. However, the most immediate challenge was recovering the evidence that had been mistakenly discarded. Cadaver dogs were dispatched to the Conestoga Landfill, where they successfully located fragments of the bones that had been thrown away that morning.

———

As Detective Gombar's team dug deeper into Michele's background, a troubling pattern emerged. Employment records revealed that Michele had maintained a close working relationship with a male colleague throughout her tenure at the healthcare agency. What wasn't apparent to most people was that Michele and this man had been conducting an intimate relationship for over a decade—a relationship conducted entirely in secret from her husband.

The Kalina marriage presented investigators with a puzzling dynamic. Jeffrey and Michele had lived essentially as care-giving partners rather than romantic spouses since 1992. Their sexual relationship had completely ceased after Elizabeth's birth in 1991, yet they continued sharing a household while Michele worked increasingly long hours to support the family financially. Jeffrey would later testify that he had not seen his wife unclothed in eighteen years, which was a detail that helped explain how Michele's pregnancies went undetected. Jeffrey's disability also prevented him from working outside the home.

Their first child, Andrew, had been born in 1987 with severe cerebral palsy and had died of natural causes in 2000 at age thirteen. The family had moved to their current apartment building in 2008, specifically because it provided housing for disabled residents.

————

Elizabeth had grown up with one absolute rule: Never enter that particular closet. Her mother had been so adamant about this prohibition that Elizabeth had never even considered challenging it until that July morning.

DNA testing would prove crucial to understanding the scope of the crimes. Laboratory analysis revealed that all five infants discovered in the closet had Michele as their biological mother. More shocking still was that at least three, possibly four of the infants had been fathered by Michele's coworker. The same man she'd been secretly involved with for years.

But the DNA evidence also revealed something that would reshape the entire investigation. There had been a sixth child —a daughter born at St. Joseph's Medical Center in Reading in October 2003. Hospital records showed Michele had given birth to this infant under her own name and immediately arranged for the child to be placed for adoption through Catholic social services. Medical staff recalled that Michele had told them she was "separated" from the baby's father.

DNA testing confirmed this surviving child was also fathered by the same coworker. Unlike the five infants found in the closet, this baby had survived and been placed legally with an adoptive family.

————

How had Michele managed to conceal six pregnancies over fourteen years from both her husband and her lover? The answer lay in Michele's carefully constructed web of medical explanations.

To both Jeffrey and her coworker, she explained periodic weight gain and physical changes as resulting from gyneco-logical problems—specifically cysts on her fallopian tubes that caused hormonal fluctuations and abdominal swelling. The medical rationalization was remarkably effective because it discouraged further inquiry from both men.

Michele had been strategic about timing her explanations. When she began showing physical signs of pregnancy, she would mention that her "cyst problems" were acting up again. Her work schedule helped maintain the deception. She often worked double shifts, spending twelve to sixteen hours away from home. Jeffrey's disability meant he rarely left the apartment and wasn't physically intimate with Michele.

When investigators questioned Michele in August 2010, she initially maintained complete innocence. She claimed she had only been pregnant twice in her life, with Andrew and Elizabeth, and denied ever experiencing miscarriages or still-births. This obvious lie, given the evidence recovered from her own closet, immediately established her pattern of deception.

When pressed further, Michele offered only hints about her alcoholism and frequent blackouts, suggesting she might not remember events clearly. She told police she had "been meaning to clean that closet," a remarkably casual reference to the storage space containing five infant corpses.

———

The forensic examination revealed crucial details about the deaths and concealment methods. At least four of the five infants had been born at or near full term, and medical examiners determined that four of them had been born alive before dying from what appeared to be asphyxia, poisoning, or neglect.

The infant encased in concrete, a male, showed clear evidence of having lived after birth. The careful preservation methods, including the concrete encasement and elaborate container storage, suggested someone who had given considerable thought to hiding these remains while maintaining access to them.

Some infants had been wrapped in multiple layers of plastic bags before being placed in containers. The methodical storage and the fact that Michele had successfully transported the remains during her family's 2008 move demonstrated a level of planning that prosecutors would later cite as evidence of premeditation.

———

Dr. Jerome Gottlieb, the forensic psychiatrist assigned to evaluate Michele's mental state, found a woman who showed no emotion whatsoever when discussing the births. She spoke about the infants as if discussing someone else's experiences, displaying complete detachment from reality.

Michele claimed to have been intoxicated during all the births, which she said had occurred in bathtubs at both her previous house and current apartment. She maintained she remembered little about the actual deliveries and initially insisted all the babies had been stillborn.

But as Dr. Gottlieb continued his evaluation, Michele's story evolved. She eventually admitted that one infant, a male, had shown clear signs of life after birth. The baby had moved, appeared to breathe, and made soft crying sounds. Michele acknowledged that she "might have wrapped the baby too tightly with a towel so that the baby couldn't breathe properly."

Defense attorney Holly Feeney argued that Michele had "learned to deny reality" due to severe physical and sexual abuse during her childhood. Dr. Gottlieb described Michele as having created what he termed a "psychological closet" where she compartmentalized traumatic memories, just as she had physically stored the infant remains.

————

Michele was initially arrested in August 2010 on charges of abuse of a corpse. By October 25, 2010, formal charges were filed: criminal homicide, aggravated assault, five counts of abuse of a corpse, five counts of concealing the death of a child, endangering the welfare of children, and reckless endangerment. She was held on a five-million-dollar bail.

The case attracted significant media attention, prompting the judge to issue a gag order in December 2010. The unusual nature of the crimes, the extended timeframe, the methodical concealment, and the functional lifestyle Michele had maintained made it unprecedented in Pennsylvania's legal history.

On August 4, 2011, Michele changed her plea to guilty on reduced charges: one count of third-degree murder for the male infant whose death could be proven to result from asphyxiation, five counts of abuse of a corpse, and five counts of concealing the death of a child.

Judge Linda K.M. Ludgate sentenced Michele to the maximum penalty: twenty to forty years in prison. During the sentencing hearing, the judge rejected defense arguments for mitigation, emphasizing that Michele had made conscious choices to continue concealing deaths.

"After the first birth and death, she could have stopped," the judge stated. "She could have sought help, could have made different choices. Instead, she concealed the death of these five babies and then wrapped them up and stored them like discarded objects."

———

The sentencing brought complicated reactions from Michele's surviving family members. Jeffrey testified that despite everything revealed about his wife's secret life, he still loved Michele and intended to remain married to her. He expressed profound regret that he hadn't known about the pregnancies, stating he would have gladly raised the children.

Elizabeth demonstrated remarkable loyalty despite the traumatic circumstances of her discovery. The nineteen-year-old described Michele as having been "a wonderful mother" and pledged to maintain contact during the prison sentence.

"She's a sweetheart. So polite, so well-spoken," Chief County Detective Michael Gombar said of Elizabeth. "She's very cooperative with us, but she loves her mother."

———

Michele Kalina is currently serving her sentence at the State Correctional Institution at Muncy, a medium-maximum security facility for women in Pennsylvania. Given her August 2011 sentencing, she would be eligible for parole consideration around 2031.

The coworker who fathered the children was never charged with any crime. Authorities determined he had no knowledge of the pregnancies or deaths. Through prosecutors, it was revealed that he wished to see the babies properly laid to rest.

The 2003 daughter who was placed for adoption is now a young adult, living with her adoptive family. For privacy reasons, little has been revealed about that child, but she represents the one life that escaped Michele's pattern of infanticide.

For the Reading community, the case remains a source of bewilderment. Mental health experts admitted they had never encountered a case quite like it. The combination of factors—multiple secret pregnancies by an older mother, the systematic concealment of remains over many years, and the ability to maintain a facade of normalcy—defied easy categorization.

"We all have theories," Detective Gombar said during the investigation. "Whether we're right or not, only she knows the answer."

The case raised disturbing questions about how such extensive deception could go undetected for so long. Michele had successfully hidden six pregnancies from her husband, daughter, coworkers, and lover while maintaining an exemplary work record and caring for her family.

For Elizabeth Kalina, the discovery in her mother's closet fundamentally changed everything she thought she knew about her family. The forbidden closet that had dominated her youth with its mysterious prohibition had finally revealed its contents, but the answers raised far more questions than they resolved.

The skeletal remains she had discovered represented siblings she had never known existed. Children who might have grown up alongside her, if circumstances had been different. The nineteen-year-old who made that first 911 call would have to live with the knowledge that her curiosity had unraveled a secret her mother had successfully maintained for more than a decade.

The five infants who died never had names, never experienced life beyond the few moments after birth. Their remains, hidden in containers for years, represented lives that were never allowed to begin. Yet Elizabeth's decision to open that forbidden closet door finally brought justice for children who never had the chance to seek it for themselves.

CHAPTER 9

THE RENO PREDATOR

B rianna Denison loved coming home to Reno. The nineteen-year-old psychology student at Santa Barbara City College cherished these winter breaks when she could reconnect with her high school friends and spend precious time with her family. Her passion for psychology stemmed from a deep desire to help people, particularly those struggling with mental health issues. Friends described her as someone who would drop every-thing to listen to someone in need.

On the evening of January 19, 2008, Brianna made plans to attend a party with friends before heading back to California for the spring semester. As the evening wound down, she made arrangements to stay at the rental house of her friend, K.T. Hunter, near the University of Nevada, Reno campus on Mackay Court. The neighborhood felt safe, the kind of place where students routinely walked alone at night and doors were often left unlocked.

Around 4 a.m., Brianna settled onto the living room couch for the night. She kicked off her shoes, placed her purse and cell phone nearby, and used a brown teddy bear as an extra pillow. The house grew quiet as K.T. headed upstairs to her bedroom, leaving Brianna to sleep peacefully in the living room. The sliding glass door remained unlocked.

―――――

K.T. Hunter's eyes opened slowly around 9 a.m. on January 20. The house felt unusually quiet as she made her way downstairs, expecting to find Brianna still sleeping on the couch, or perhaps already awake and making coffee in the kitchen. However, Brianna was gone.

K.T. called out Brianna's name, thinking her friend might have moved to another room during the night. The silence that greeted her was absolute and unsettling. She checked the bathroom, the kitchen, and even looked outside, but Brianna's shoes remained exactly where she'd left them the night before. Her purse sat untouched on the side table, wallet and identification still inside. Her cell phone lay silent next to it, fully charged and showing no missed calls or messages.

Something was very wrong.

K.T. approached the couch where Brianna had been sleeping, her heart beginning to race. The pillow showed a small but distinct bloodstain about the size of a silver dollar, dark red against the pale fabric. The brown teddy bear Brianna had been using as an extra pillow was nowhere to be found. The blanket was rumpled and pushed aside, as if there had been some kind of struggle.

Her hands shaking, K.T. reached for her phone and called Brianna's parents first, then immediately contacted the police. The blood, the missing items, the abandoned personal belongings—everything pointed to something terrible having happened in the predawn hours while K.T. slept upstairs, completely unaware.

————

Reno Police arrived at the house within minutes. The first responders took one look at the scene and immediately called for detectives and crime scene technicians. The unlocked door, the bloodstain, the missing personal items— everything pointed to an abduction.

Detectives surveyed the scene with growing concern. The evidence spoke for itself: Brianna Denison had not left voluntarily. Her shoes, purse, and phone remained behind while she vanished into the early morning darkness wearing only her clothes and socks. The bloodstain on the pillow suggested she had been injured, and the missing teddy bear indicated that her attacker had taken something with him. Most unsettling of all, K.T. mentioned that her dog had never barked during the night. It suggested either that the intruder was someone the animal recognized, or that he had moved with extraordinary stealth.

Crime scene technicians processed the house methodically. They photographed the bloodstain, collected the pillow for laboratory analysis, and dusted for fingerprints. On the front door handle, they discovered touch DNA from an unidenti- fied male, someone who had no legitimate reason to be in that house.

By January 21, the FBI had joined the search effort, their involvement signaling that this was far more serious than a typical missing person case. The police held a press confer- ence, treating the case as an apparent kidnapping from the very beginning.

The community response was immediate and overwhelming. Electronic casino marquees throughout Reno displayed Brianna's photograph alongside desperate pleas for information. Billboards went up across the city. The phrase "Bring Bri Back" became a rallying cry, accompanied by royal blue ribbons—Brianna's favorite color—tied to trees, cars, and lampposts throughout the area.

———

As investigators dug deeper into Brianna's disappearance, they began examining other recent crimes in the area. The University of Nevada, Reno campus, and surrounding neighborhoods had been on edge for months due to a series of unsolved sexual assaults.

The first attack had occurred in October 2007, when a woman was raped at gunpoint in a campus parking garage. The victim had initially chosen not to report the crime, but the publicity surrounding Brianna's case prompted her to come forward.

On November 13, 2007, another woman had been battered and sexually assaulted. The attacker had been described as a white male, approximately twenty-eight to forty years old, with brown hair and a lean but muscular build.

The most recent assault before Brianna's disappearance had occurred on December 16, 2007. A woman was kidnapped, sexually assaulted, and then brought back to her home by her attacker. This victim provided detailed descriptions of both the perpetrator and his vehicle—an extended-cab pickup truck with distinctive interior features including a dome light above the windshield, a floor-mounted console, and carpeted floor mats. Most memorably, she recalled seeing a baby's shoe on the floorboard.

Crime lab technicians made a chilling discovery when they compared DNA evidence from these cases. The male DNA found at Brianna's abduction scene matched samples from the November and December assaults perfectly. The investigators were dealing with a serial predator operating in their community, someone who was escalating his behavior and becoming increasingly bold.

On January 29, authorities released a composite sketch based on the previous victims' descriptions. The suspect was described as a white male between twenty-eight and forty years old, over 5'6" tall, with a long face, square chin, and brown hair. Victims noted he appeared physically fit and had shaved his pubic area, suggesting he was methodical about eliminating physical evidence.

———

Hundreds of volunteers joined the search for Brianna as January 2008 drew to a close. Search teams spread across Reno and its outskirts, braving harsh winter conditions as they combed through snowy fields, dense brush, and along the Truckee River. The volunteers came from all walks of life, including Nevada's First Lady, Dawn Gibbons, who personally crawled through sagebrush and snow alongside other searchers.

Meanwhile, investigators followed every lead that came in through the tip lines. They interviewed nearly one hundred registered sex offenders living within a mile of the Mackay Courthouse, conducting thorough background checks and verifying alibis for each one.

As days turned into weeks without any sign of Brianna, hope began to fade among her family and friends. Her mother, Bridgette, maintained a vigil of sorts, appearing at press conferences and search gatherings, always wearing royal blue in honor of her daughter.

————

February 15, 2008, started as an ordinary Friday for Albert Jimenez. The Reno resident was returning to work from his lunch break when something caught his eye in a vacant lot near a light industrial area. Among some discarded tree limbs and brush, he noticed what appeared to be bright orange fabric.

Jimenez moved closer to investigate. The orange fabric turned out to be socks on what resembled human feet. His first thought was that someone had dumped a department store mannequin, but as he looked more carefully, he saw exposed teeth and what appeared to be a bloody wound on the body's shoulder.

His heart racing, Jimenez ran back to his workplace and called the police immediately.

Officers arrived within minutes and secured the scene. The body was found lying in a shallow depression, partially concealed by debris that included an old Christmas tree that had been placed over it. Heavy snowfall in recent weeks had likely helped hide the remains from view.

The victim was nude except for the bright orange socks. The location was approximately eight miles from the Mackay Courthouse, where Brianna had been abducted.

The body was soon confirmed to be Brianna Denison, ending the twenty-six-day search in the worst possible way.

———

The medical examiner conducted Brianna's autopsy on February 16. The findings painted a horrific picture of the young woman's final hours. Brianna had been sexually assaulted and strangled to death, with ligature marks around her neck indicating she had been killed using some kind of fabric as a garrote.

The crime scene revealed additional disturbing evidence. Near Brianna's body, investigators found two pairs of women's thong underwear, neither of which belonged to her. The presence of these items suggested that her killer collected trophies from his victims.

The first pair was pink and petite-sized, found wrapped around Brianna's neck. The elastic band matched the pattern of ligature marks on Brianna's throat perfectly. She had been strangled with it. DNA testing revealed genetic material from three individuals: Brianna herself, her friend K.T. Hunter, and an unknown male.

The second pair was even more disturbing. Black with pink hearts and images of the Pink Panther cartoon character, this set of underwear was several sizes too large to be Brianna's. They contained DNA from the same unknown male suspect and from another unidentified female. This appeared to be a trophy from another victim, possibly someone who had not yet reported an attack.

Police published photographs and detailed descriptions of the Pink Panther underwear, urging any woman who was missing such underwear to come forward. They suspected it might lead them to another victim who had not reported her assault.

All of the DNA evidence confirmed what investigators already suspected—the same perpetrator was responsible for Brianna's murder and the previous sexual assaults. The killer was definitely a serial predator, and he was still at large.

———

With Brianna's body recovered and the cause of death established, the investigation shifted into high gear. The case was featured on the television show, America's Most Wanted, and over 5,000 tips poured in through various hotlines. Investigators collected DNA samples from more than 700 men who volunteered to be tested, hoping to find a match.

University officials increased campus security patrols and implemented new safety protocols. Students traveled in groups more frequently, and local stores reported a surge in sales of pepper spray, stun guns, and small handguns as people sought to protect themselves.

The community's determination to find Brianna's killer was unwavering. Vigils continued throughout the spring and summer, with hundreds of people gathering to remember Brianna and demand justice. Royal blue ribbons became more prominent throughout the city, a constant reminder that a predator walked among them.

Investigators knew they were looking for someone familiar with the university area—someone who understood the rhythms and patterns of student life. But as spring turned to summer, then summer to fall, the case remained frustratingly unsolved.

On November 1, 2008, almost ten months after Brianna's murder, a phone call to the Secret Witness tip line changed everything. The caller was a friend of a woman named Carleen Harmon, and she had information that would finally break the case open.

According to the tipster, Harmon had confided that she had discovered a pair of women's thong underwear in the glove compartment of her boyfriend's truck—underwear that didn't belong to her. The boyfriend's name was James Michael Biela, and given the widely publicized details about the underwear found at Brianna's crime scene, the discovery had the potential to be the break investigators had been desperately seeking.

James Biela

Research into James Biela revealed details that made investigators' hearts race. Biela was a twenty-seven-year-old former Marine who worked as a pipefitter in construction. He lived in nearby Sparks, Nevada, with Carleen Harmon and their four-year-old son.

More significantly, Biela owned an extended-cab pickup truck that matched the description provided by the December 2007 assault victim. Even more intriguingly, he had moved to Washington state in March 2008, shortly after Brianna's murder, for a construction job, only returning to Nevada in the fall. This timeline aligned perfectly with the cessation of attacks in the Reno area.

When detectives approached Biela for questioning in mid-November 2008, his behavior immediately raised red flags. He denied any involvement in the crimes, but more significantly, he flatly refused to provide a DNA sample for comparison testing.

Investigators interviewed Carleen Harmon separately, assuming she would provide an alibi for Biela during the times of the attacks. Instead, Harmon delivered devastating testimony. She told detectives she could not account for his whereabouts during the early morning hours of December 16, 2007, or January 20, 2008, the exact times when the December assault and Brianna's abduction had occurred.

Harmon described her relationship with Biela as tumultuous. He would sometimes disappear for days at a time without explanation. When confronted about the thong underwear found in his truck, she admitted it had troubled her deeply.

Faced with Biela's refusal to provide DNA, investigators proposed an innovative approach. With Carleen's consent, they could obtain a DNA sample from the couple's four-year-old son. Familial DNA testing could determine whether Biela could be excluded as the source of the crime scene DNA.

Carleen, perhaps finally recognizing the full severity of the situation, agreed to help with the investigation.

———

The results of the familial DNA testing were unequivocal. The four-year-old boy's genetic profile indicated that his biological father could not be ruled out as the source of the DNA evidence collected from Brianna's crime scene and the previous assault scenes.

Armed with this probable cause, investigators obtained warrants for Biela's arrest. On the morning of November 12, 2008, officers moved in for the arrest that would finally bring justice for Brianna Denison.

Biela was apprehended in the parking lot of the Stepping Stones children's daycare center in Reno, where he was dropping off his son. The arrest was executed smoothly, with Biela offering no resistance.

He was booked into the Washoe County Jail on charges of first-degree murder, first-degree kidnapping, and sexual assault in connection with Brianna's case, as well as sexual assault charges for the previous attacks.

When Biela finally provided a direct DNA sample following his arrest, the results confirmed what the familial testing had already indicated. His DNA was a perfect match for the genetic material found at all the crime scenes, conclusively linking him to Brianna's murder and the series of sexual assaults.

The investigation revealed additional disturbing details about Biela's background. He had been discharged from the Marines under less-than-honorable circumstances, reportedly due to drug use. In 2001, he had been arrested for threatening an ex-girlfriend's neighbor with a knife.

The truck Biela had owned during the time of the attacks was located in Idaho and recovered as evidence. Forensic examination confirmed that it matched the descriptions provided by the December 2007 victim in remarkable detail.

————

James Biela's trial began in May 2010, nearly two and a half years after Brianna's murder. The prosecution's case was built on irrefutable DNA evidence and powerful testimony from survivors.

Carleen Harmon testified about finding the thong underwear in Biela's truck and her inability to account for his whereabouts during the time of the attacks. The October 2007 victim positively identified Biela in court as the man who had raped her at gunpoint. The December 2007 victim described her kidnapping and assault in harrowing detail.

The medical examiner testified about Brianna's autopsy results, explaining how the pink thong underwear had been used as a ligature to strangle the young woman. Crime lab technicians presented the DNA evidence that linked Biela to all the crimes.

Biela's defense team faced a nearly impossible task given the overwhelming evidence. They focused on arguing for mercy during the penalty phase, during which they presented evidence of Biela's troubled childhood, where he had witnessed his father's regular physical abuse of his mother.

On May 27, 2010, after approximately nine hours of deliberation, the jury returned guilty verdicts on all counts. Biela was convicted of first-degree murder for Brianna's killing, as well as kidnapping and sexual assault charges related to all three victims.

During the penalty phase, prosecutors argued that Biela posed a continuing threat to society and that the death penalty was the only appropriate punishment. The jury agreed, unanimously sentencing Biela to death for Brianna's murder.

Judge Robert Perry imposed additional consecutive life sentences for the other felony counts, ensuring that even if the death sentence were ever overturned, Biela would never walk free.

———

The resolution of Brianna Denison's murder case sparked important changes that would honor her memory and potentially save other lives. Bridgette Denison converted her anguish into a mission for criminal justice reforms that could prevent other families from experiencing the devastating loss she had endured.

Her primary focus became promoting legislation that would expand DNA collection from arrestees, not just those convicted of crimes. The push was driven by a heartbreaking realization: If DNA collection laws had been different, James Biela might have been identified and stopped before he'd ever had the chance to harm Brianna. He had been arrested on a felony charge in 1996, but DNA collection was not required for arrestees at that time.

Senate Bill 243, known as "Brianna's Law," passed the Nevada Legislature in 2013. The law requires DNA collection from anyone arrested for a felony offense, not just those ultimately convicted. The legislation includes important privacy protections, requiring that DNA records be destroyed if charges are dropped or the person is acquitted.

Since its implementation, Brianna's Law has helped solve numerous cold cases throughout Nevada and has freed several people who were wrongfully convicted. The law has become a model for other states, contributing to national conversations about DNA databases and their role in both solving crimes and protecting the innocent.

James Biela remains on death row at Ely State Prison, his appeals exhausted. In 2019, the Nevada Supreme Court denied his final appeal, upholding both his conviction and death sentence.

———

The pain for Brianna's family would continue in unexpected ways. Ten years after Brianna's murder, her cousin Caitlin Denison disappeared under circumstances that would haunt the family once again. On January 9, 2018, Caitlin flew from Reno to Midland, Texas, to meet a man she had encountered previously—a truck driver working in the Permian Basin oil industry whose name she had never shared with her family.

After landing in Midland, Caitlin stayed with the man in his RV before contacting family and friends on January 10, 2018, to say she was at a Walmart with the man but was "afraid for her life." Investigators believe the pair also visited a Domino's Pizza and Rick's Cabaret that day before Caitlin vanished without a trace. Like Brianna, Caitlin was nineteen years old when she disappeared. The case is still unsolved.

CHAPTER 10
FOX HOLLOW FARM

The thirteen-year-old boy wandered through the wooded area behind his family's sprawling estate, kicking at fallen leaves and broken branches. Fox Hollow Farm stretched across eighteen acres of pristine Indiana countryside, and Erich Baumeister had spent countless hours exploring every corner of the property since his family moved there three years earlier. The Tudor-style mansion with its indoor swimming pool felt like a castle compared to their previous home, and the woods provided endless adventure for a curious teenager.

But on this crisp October afternoon in 1994, Erich stumbled upon something that would haunt him for the rest of his life.

Half-buried beneath a pile of decomposing leaves, a human skull stared back at him through empty sockets. Erich's heart pounded as he noticed other bones scattered nearby—a femur here, ribs there—all bleached white by the elements. His hands trembling, he gathered up the skull and several other bones before racing back to the house.

"Mom! Mom!" he shouted as he burst through the back door, still clutching his macabre discovery. "I found bones in the woods!"

Julie Baumeister looked up from the kitchen counter where she had been preparing dinner. Her son stood in the doorway, dirt streaking his clothes, holding what was unmistakably a human skull. For a moment, time seemed suspended as mother and son stared at each other in stunned silence.

"Where did you find this?" Julie managed to ask, her voice barely above a whisper.

Erich led his mother to the spot where he had made the discovery. Julie's stomach churned as she saw the additional bones scattered throughout the area. This wasn't some animal carcass or ancient burial ground. These were human remains, and they were on her family's property.

When Herbert Baumeister returned home that evening, Julie confronted him with their son's disturbing find. Herb examined the skull with surprising calm, turning it over in his hands as if he were inspecting a piece of pottery at one of his thrift stores.

"It's nothing to worry about," he said matter-of-factly. "These are medical specimens. Remember, my father was an anesthesiologist. He had a skeleton for his studies. I must have disposed of it out here and forgotten about it."

Julie felt a wave of relief wash over her. Of course. Dr. Herbert Baumeister had practiced medicine for decades before his death in 1986. It made perfect sense that he would have owned medical teaching materials. Within a few days, Julie noticed the bones had disappeared from the woods, presumably scattered by animals.

The incident faded from her memory as life continued its normal rhythm at Fox Hollow Farm.

———

Detective Mary Wilson of the Indianapolis Metropolitan Police Department spread the missing person reports across her desk, searching for patterns that might connect the cases. Since May 1993, ten young men had vanished from the Indianapolis area under remarkably similar circumstances. All were in their twenties or thirties. All had last been seen at gay bars in the downtown district. All had simply disappeared without a trace.

The families of these missing men painted pictures of vibrant lives cut short. Roger Goodlet, thirty-three, worked as a counselor and was described by friends as outgoing and responsible. Steven Hale, twenty-six, had moved to Indianapolis for a fresh start and was building a new life for himself. Richard Hamilton, only twenty, was a nursing student with dreams of helping others. Jeffrey Jones, thirty-one, was known for his quick wit and generous spirit.

Each disappearance followed an eerily similar pattern. The men would go out for an evening at one of Indianapolis's popular gay establishments—venues like the 501 Tavern or Our Place. They would be seen talking to someone, perhaps sharing drinks or dancing. Then they would leave, and no one would ever see them again.

Detective Wilson recognized that these weren't random disappearances. Someone was hunting these men, using the relative anonymity of the bar scene to select victims. However, identifying a suspect seemed impossible when the perpetrator could blend into the crowd and leave no witnesses behind.

———

The breakthrough came from an unexpected source—a man who had narrowly escaped becoming a victim himself.

Mark Goodyear had been frequenting Indianapolis's gay bars for years, but his encounter with "Brian Smart" in the summer of 1994 left him deeply shaken. Mark had met the man at a downtown establishment, where Brian had struck up a conversation and invited him to continue the evening at his mansion outside the city.

Brian had seemed nervous, constantly looking over his shoulder as if worried about being recognized. Despite this odd behavior, Mark had agreed to accompany him to what turned out to be an impressive estate with an indoor swimming pool. The pool area was decorated in a bizarre fashion—mannequins positioned around tables and chairs as if they were guests at a party.

As the evening progressed, Brian encouraged Mark to drink heavily, constantly refilling his glass with strong cocktails. Something about his host's insistence made Mark uncomfortable, so he began secretly pouring out his drinks and refilling the glass with water when Brian wasn't looking.

They eventually moved to the pool, where Brian suggested they try some 'enhanced' sexual activities involving erotic asphyxiation—the dangerous practice of restricting oxygen flow to the brain during sex to intensify arousal. Mark went along initially, but as Brian's grip around his neck tightened, survival instincts kicked in. He sensed that Brian was pushing far beyond safe limits, using a pool hose and later a belt to increase the pressure around Mark's throat.

"If I had been severely under the influence, he probably would have gone further," Mark later told investigators. "It made me believe that he has done this before."

Mark managed to break free and insist they stop. Brian seemed disappointed but didn't press the issue. The rest of the evening passed without incident, but Mark left with the unsettling conviction that he had narrowly escaped serious harm, even death.

Months passed before Mark saw Brian again. He had warned friends in the gay community to be on the lookout for a man matching Brian's description, but the predator had seemingly vanished. In November 1995, Mark spotted the same man at a downtown bar and watched as he left with another patron. This time, Mark followed them to the parking lot and managed to write down the license plate number of Brian's Buick before the car disappeared into the night.

Mark immediately contacted the police, providing them with the plate number and a detailed description of his encounter. Detective Wilson ran the plates through the Bureau of Motor Vehicles database, and the results surprised everyone involved in the investigation.

The car was registered to Herbert Richard Baumeister of Westfield, Indiana.

————

Herbert Baumeister seemed an unlikely suspect for serial murder. At forty-eight years old, he was a successful businessman who owned two Sav-A-Lot thrift stores in

Indianapolis. He lived with his wife, Julie, and their three children on a beautiful estate in one of the area's most affluent suburbs. Neighbors described the family as private but pleasant, noting that Herb took an active role in his children's lives, even packing their school lunches each morning.

Herbert Baumeister

Born in 1947, Herb had grown up in a middle-class Indianapolis family. His father was a respected anesthesiologist, and the family seemed to embody middle-American values. But beneath this conventional exterior, disturbing patterns had emerged early in Herb's life.

During his teenage years, classmates recalled his bizarre behavior. He'd had an obsession with urine, sometimes urinating on teachers' desks or in other inappropriate locations. He also enjoyed playing with dead animals and had once left a dead crow on a teacher's desk. These incidents had alarmed his parents enough that they'd had him evaluated at a psychiatric hospital, where he had been diagnosed with paranoid schizophrenia and antisocial personality disorder.

Despite these early warning signs, Herb managed to function in society. He attended Indiana University briefly, though he never completed a degree. In 1971, he married Julie Saiter, whom he had met in college. The couple appeared to have a stable if reserved relationship. Julie later revealed that their physical intimacy was extremely limited—they were intimate only five or six times during their entire twenty-five-year marriage, and she had never seen her husband naked.

Herb's professional life was marked by both success and troubling incidents. He initially worked for the Indiana Bureau of Motor Vehicles, where supervisors noted his perfectionist tendencies and sudden, unprovoked rages. His employment ended abruptly in 1985 when he was fired for urinating on a letter addressed to the governor. Around the same time, he was arrested for a hit-and-run incident, then later for conspiracy to commit theft, though both charges were eventually dropped.

After losing his BMV job, Herb spent time in psychiatric care before launching his business venture with Julie. The Sav-A-Lot stores proved remarkably successful, allowing the family to live comfortably and eventually purchase Fox Hollow Farm in 1991.

What investigators didn't initially know was that Herb had been living a double life for years. While presenting himself as a devoted family man and conservative businessman, he had been secretly frequenting gay bars in downtown Indianapolis. Patrons at these establishments remembered him as awkward and nervous, always seeming worried about being recognized.

When Detective Wilson approached Herb in November 1995 to question him about the missing men, he vehemently denied any involvement and refused to allow a search of his property. Without physical evidence linking him to the crimes, police couldn't obtain a search warrant, and the investigation stalled.

Wilson then approached Julie Baumeister, hoping to gain her cooperation. She met with detectives at one of the thrift stores, where they delicately explained that her husband was a suspect in multiple disappearances. They revealed his secret visits to gay bars and asked for permission to search Fox Hollow Farm.

Julie was devastated. She had no idea about her husband's double life, and the accusations seemed impossible to believe. She confronted Herb that night, and he flatly denied everything. Choosing to believe her husband, Julie told the police they were wrong and refused to cooperate with the investigation.

———

By early 1996, the Baumeister marriage was unraveling. The thrift store business had begun to struggle financially, and the couple's relationship grew increasingly strained. In January, Julie filed for divorce, and Herb moved out of their shared bedroom. They barely spoke to each other, and when they did, conversations often erupted into arguments.

Julie couldn't shake her doubts about the police accusations. The memory of the skull Erich had found in 1994 began to gnaw at her. Her husband's explanation about medical specimens had seemed reasonable at the time, but now she wondered if there might be another explanation. As spring turned to summer, her fears intensified. Herb's behavior became increasingly erratic.

The breaking point came in June 1996. Julie realized she could no longer ignore the possibility that the police might be right about her husband. When Herb left town on a business trip in late June, she contacted her attorney and then called the Hamilton County Sheriff's Department. For the first time since the investigation began, she gave permission for authorities to search Fox Hollow Farm.

———

On June 24, 1996, Detective Mary Wilson and a team of investigators drove through the gates of Fox Hollow Farm. The property was even more impressive than they had imagined—eighteen acres of rolling hills, mature trees, and manicured lawns surrounding an elegant Tudor mansion. It seemed impossible that such a peaceful, affluent setting could harbor the dark secrets they suspected.

Julie led them to the wooded area behind the house where Erich had found the skull two years earlier. The investigators began a careful search, looking for any signs of human remains or evidence of criminal activity.

They didn't have to look long.

Within minutes of beginning their search, officers spotted what appeared to be burned bone fragments scattered on the ground. Nearby, they found an intact human foot, the bones still articulated together. As they expanded their search area, more horrifying discoveries emerged: additional bone fragments, some charred black from fire, as well as metal handcuff hinges and spent shotgun shells.

The implications were immediately clear. Fox Hollow Farm had been used as a disposal site for human remains, and the killer had attempted to destroy evidence by burning the bodies.

Word of the discovery spread quickly through law enforcement channels. The Hamilton County Sheriff's Department secured the property and called in forensic experts from the University of Indianapolis. For the next several weeks, teams of archaeologists and anthropologists methodically excavated and sifted through the soil in the wooded areas.

What they uncovered defied imagination. More than ten thousand bone fragments and teeth were recovered from various locations around the property. Many of the bones showed evidence of both burning and deliberate breakage, suggesting the killer had gone to extraordinary lengths to destroy the bodies and prevent the identification of his victims.

The fragmented nature of the remains made the forensic team's job enormously difficult. Bones had been burned at high temperatures, then crushed and scattered across multiple sites. Some fragments were no larger than a fingernail. Despite these challenges, experts determined that the remains represented at least eleven different individuals.

As the excavation continued, investigators began to piece together what had happened at Fox Hollow Farm. The pattern of disappearances matched times when Julie and the children were away at their lake condominium, leaving Herb alone on the property. The indoor swimming pool, with its bizarre mannequin decorations, appeared to be one of the primary crime scenes. The remote wooded areas had served as both killing grounds and burial sites.

By September 1996, forensic analysts had managed to iden- tify three of the victims through dental records and DNA comparisons: Roger Goodlet, Steven Hale, and Richard Hamilton. All were men who had disappeared from Indianapolis gay bars between 1993 and 1994. All had been in their twenties or thirties. All had simply vanished without a trace until their remains were discovered at Fox Hollow Farm.

But by the time investigators were ready to arrest Herbert Baumeister, he was gone.

———

Herb had learned about the search of his property, possibly through his attorney or through news reports. Realizing that his carefully constructed double life was about to be exposed, he fled Indiana in late June 1996. An arrest warrant was issued on June 29, but by then, he had already crossed the border into Canada.

For several days, law enforcement agencies on both sides of the border searched for the fugitive businessman. His face appeared on wanted posters and news broadcasts. Tips poured in from citizens who thought they had spotted him, but each lead proved false.

On July 3, 1996, campers at Pinery Provincial Park in Ontario, Canada, made a grim discovery. A car was parked near a wooded picnic area, and lying on the ground about twenty feet away was the body of a middle-aged man. He had been shot once in the head with a .357 Magnum revolver.

Canadian authorities quickly identified the deceased as Herbert Richard Baumeister. The suspected serial killer had become his own final victim.

Near Baumeister's body, investigators found a three-page suicide note. In it, he expressed despair over his failing marriage and the financial problems that had plagued his business. He apologized to his wife and children for the pain he had caused them through his personal failures.

Remarkably, the note made no mention of the murder investigation, the bodies found on his property, or any remorse for the crimes he was accused of committing. It was as if he couldn't or wouldn't acknowledge the horrific acts that had brought law enforcement to his door.

With Baumeister's death, the criminal case effectively ended. There would be no trial, no confession, and no opportunity for the victims' families to confront their loved ones' killer. He would never face a courtroom. No jury. No verdict. No apology.

The investigation shifted focus to identifying the remaining victims and understanding the full scope of his crimes.

———

As investigators delved deeper into Baumeister's background, a disturbing picture emerged of crimes that stretched back more than a decade. Between 1980 and 1991, at least eleven young men had been found dead along the Interstate 70 corridor in Indiana and Ohio. These victims, dubbed the "I-70 Strangler" cases, had been discovered in rural areas, streams, and ditches, all having died by strangulation.

The similarities to the Fox Hollow Farm murders were striking. The I-70 victims were typically young men, often from marginalized communities. They were usually found partially clothed or naked, and their bodies were dumped in remote locations. Like the later victims, they had been strangled to death.

Police noticed that the I-70 murders had stopped in 1991—the same year Baumeister had purchased Fox Hollow Farm. The timing suggested that he had simply changed his disposal methods, using his private property instead of public dumping grounds.

Witnesses from some of the earlier cases helped confirm the connection. In 1983, a man had seen a suspect leave a gay bar with Michael Riley, one of the I-70 victims. Years later, that witness positively identified a photograph of Herbert Baumeister as the same man he had seen that night.

In April 1998, authorities formally announced their belief that Baumeister was responsible for at least nine of the I-70 murders. Combined with the Fox Hollow Farm victims, his total victim count could exceed twenty people, making him one of the most prolific serial killers in Indiana history.

———

The investigation of Herbert Baumeister's crimes didn't end with his death. For decades, forensic experts continued working to identify the remaining victims found at Fox Hollow Farm. The task was made enormously difficult by the condition of the remains—many bones had been burned beyond recognition, then deliberately broken into tiny fragments.

By the late 1990s, authorities had identified four victims using the DNA technology available at the time. However, budget constraints forced them to suspend the identification efforts, leaving several victims nameless.

————

The case remained largely dormant until 2022, when Eric Pranger contacted the Hamilton County Coroner's office through Facebook. His cousin, Allen Livingston, had disappeared in 1993, and Pranger suspected he might be among Baumeister's victims. This inquiry prompted newly elected Coroner Jeff Jellison to launch a renewed identification effort using advanced DNA techniques and forensic genetic genealogy.

The modern investigation has begun to bear fruit. In October 2023, Allen Livingston was identified as the ninth known victim from Fox Hollow Farm. His identification brought some measure of closure to his family, particularly his mother, Sharon, who had spent thirty years wondering what happened to her son. She died just one month after learning the truth about Allen's fate.

Additional identifications followed. Manuel Resendez was confirmed as another victim in January 2024, and Jeffrey Jones was identified in May 2024. Further efforts throughout the 2020s added five more identified victims to the original four from the 1990s. As of early 2025, forensic scientists have extracted DNA profiles from multiple victims, though several remain unidentified.

The renewed investigation has revealed the human cost of Baumeister's crimes in harsh detail. Many of his victims were marginalized individuals whose disappearances weren't taken seriously by authorities at the time. Some may have been estranged from their families or ostracized because of their sexuality. Their murders robbed the world of teachers, counselors, students, and countless other individuals who had dreams and aspirations beyond the brutal circumstances of their deaths.

In August 2024, a memorial was dedicated to Baumeister's identified victims in Westfield, Indiana. The memorial features a plaque with the names of the nine confirmed victims and space for additional names as more identifications are made. Family members gathered to remember their loved ones and to witness the interment of cremated remains that had been stored in evidence for nearly three decades.

The investigation continues, with forensic experts working to extract DNA from thousands of bone fragments still in storage. Each identification brings answers to families who have waited decades for the truth. Each name restored to a victim represents a small victory over the evil that Herbert Baumeister brought to Fox Hollow Farm.

The property itself has taken on an almost mythical quality in local folklore. Current owners report strange occurrences and unexplained phenomena, leading to speculation about paranormal activity. Whether or not one believes in such things, Fox Hollow Farm remains a place where unimaginable evil once flourished beneath a facade of suburban respectability.

CHAPTER 11

THE JACK IN THE BOX MURDERS

The late shift at Jack in the Box on Main Street and Lindsay Road in Mesa, Arizona, was supposed to be routine. Three employees worked the graveyard hours that warm Sunday night in May 2002: Kenneth Brown, a twenty-seven-year-old with an easy smile; Beatriz "Betty" Alvarado, thirty-one, known for her reliability; and thirty-year-old Fausto Jimenez, who had recently been promoted to assistant-manager-in-training. By 10:00 p.m., the dining room was locked according to company policy, leaving only the drive-thru window open for late-night customers.

The three had settled into their familiar rhythm. Kenneth handled the grill, Betty worked the drive-through window and register, while Fausto supervised operations from his assistant-manager-in-training position. The restaurant hummed with the quiet efficiency of a well-oiled machine, the kind of peaceful monotony that made the night shift bearable.

None of them heard the knock at the locked front door at first.

When the sound came again, more insistent this time, Fausto looked up from his paperwork. Through the glass, he could make out a familiar figure—someone wearing a Jack in the Box uniform just like theirs. The young man outside appeared agitated, gesturing urgently at the door.

Fausto recognized him immediately. Christopher Hargrave had worked at this same location just weeks earlier, though his employment had ended abruptly after some trouble with the cash register. Seeing him now in uniform, claiming through the glass that he'd been "called into work" unexpectedly, Fausto felt a moment of confusion. He hadn't heard anything about additional staff being scheduled.

But Hargrave seemed desperate, and mistakes happened with scheduling all the time. Against his better judgment, Fausto walked to the front door and turned the lock.

Christopher Allen Hargrave stepped inside with a tight smile. At twenty years old, he carried himself with an intensity that seemed disproportionate to his slight frame. His pale blue eyes swept the restaurant interior as if cataloging every detail. Behind him, the Arizona night stretched dark and empty.

"Thanks, man," Hargrave said, his voice carrying an edge that hadn't been there during his previous employment. "Glad you guys are here."

Fausto nodded, though something felt off about the entire situation. Before he could ask any questions about the supposed schedule change, another figure appeared at the still-open door.

Steve Boggs stepped into the restaurant with the confident stride of someone who belonged there. At twenty-one, he was slightly older than Hargrave but carried himself with the same coiled tension. His hand rested conspicuously behind his back as his eyes met those of the three employees.

In that moment, the atmosphere in the Jack in the Box shifted from routine to something far more dangerous.

"Nobody move," Boggs commanded, his voice cutting through the ambient hum of the kitchen equipment. His hand emerged from behind his back, revealing a .45-caliber handgun that gleamed under the fluorescent lights.

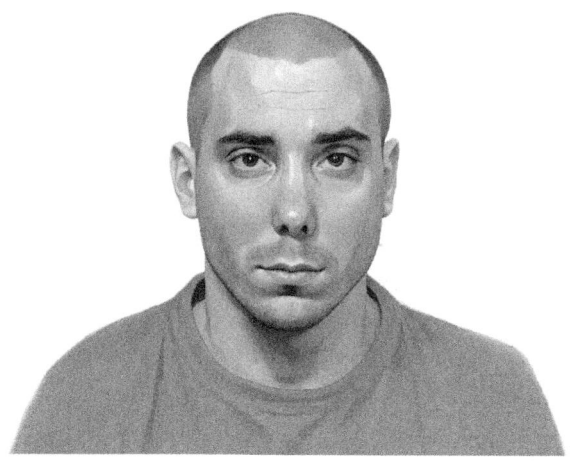

Steve Boggs

Kenneth dropped the spatula he'd been holding. Betty stepped back from the register, her eyes wide with shock. Fausto felt his stomach drop as he realized the magnitude of his mistake in opening that door.

"Get on the ground," Boggs ordered, waving the weapon toward the three employees. "Face down, hands where I can see them."

The three workers complied immediately, lowering them-selves to the cold tile floor of the restaurant. Their hearts pounded as they pressed their faces against the ground, trying to process what was happening to their quiet Sunday night.

Hargrave moved with practiced efficiency, his earlier nervousness replaced by focused determination. He positioned himself as a lookout while Boggs approached the cash registers. The sound of the drawers being forced open echoed through the restaurant as Boggs rifled through the contents.

"Empty your pockets," Boggs barked at the prone employees. "Wallets, keys, everything."

Kenneth, Betty, and Fausto fumbled to comply, removing their personal belongings and sliding them across the floor. The small pile of items seemed pathetic under the harsh lights—a few dollars in cash, some credit cards, car keys.

Boggs finished with the registers, his face showing disappointment at the meager take. Late Sunday nights were never big money shifts, and the total haul looked to be less than three hundred dollars. But money, it seemed, wasn't the only item on the agenda.

———

"Get up," Hargrave commanded, his voice now matching his partner's harsh tone. "Slowly."

The three employees rose to their feet, keeping their hands visible. They stood clustered together near the counter, uncertain what would come next but hoping desperately that cooperation would see them through the ordeal.

Boggs gestured toward the back of the restaurant with his weapon. "Move. Toward the kitchen."

Kenneth, Betty, and Fausto exchanged glances before beginning to walk slowly toward the back. Their footsteps seemed unnaturally loud on the tile floor as they passed through the kitchen area, past the familiar equipment they'd worked with countless times, until they reached the walk-in cooler. The heavy door stood open, revealing the white interior where food was stored during off-hours.

"Inside," Hargrave ordered.

The three employees hesitated for a moment, some primal instinct warning them against entering the confined space. But the gun in Boggs's hand left no room for argument. They stepped into the cooler, their breath beginning to fog in the chilled air.

"Further back," Boggs commanded. "Into the freezer."

At the rear of the cooler, another door led to an even smaller, colder space—the restaurant's freezer, where frozen products were stored. The metal walls seemed to close in around them as they were herded into the cramped compartment.

"Get down on your knees," Boggs ordered, his voice echoing strangely in the confined space.

Kenneth, Betty, and Fausto lowered themselves to the freezer floor, the cold seeping through their uniforms. They knelt facing away from their captors, their hands clasped behind their heads as instructed.

The freezer fell silent except for the hum of the refrigeration unit. The three employees waited, hoping against hope that their ordeal was nearly over—that the two men would simply lock them inside and flee with their small haul of cash.

Instead, Boggs raised his weapon.

The first gunshot exploded in the confined space with deafening intensity. Then another. And another. The .45-caliber rounds tore through the freezer air as Boggs methodically fired at each of the kneeling figures.

Kenneth crumpled immediately, his body still. Betty cried out as bullets struck her back, the impact sending her sprawling across the freezer floor. Fausto felt the searing pain of multiple rounds hitting him, his vision blurring as he collapsed.

But the shooting didn't stop there. As Boggs fired, his voice rose in a crescendo of racial epithets, the hateful words echoing off the metal walls of the freezer. The attack wasn't just robbery—it was an execution fueled by ideology and rage.

Hargrave stepped forward and fired the weapon at least once himself, adding his shot to the massacre in the confined space while Boggs continued his methodical execution of the three victims. Shell casings clattered to the freezer floor as the two men emptied their fury into the bodies of their victims.

When the gunfire finally ceased, an eerie quiet settled over the freezer. Boggs and Hargrave stood amid the carnage they had created, their breathing heavy in the cold air. Below them, the three employees lay motionless on the floor, blood pooling beneath their bodies.

Satisfied with their work, the two killers turned and walked out of the freezer, leaving their victims for dead. They made their way back through the restaurant, gathering up the money from the registers and the personal items from their victims.

As they prepared to leave, a sound stopped them cold. Screaming from the direction of the freezer. Someone was still alive.

Boggs cursed and turned back toward the rear of the restaurant. He couldn't afford to leave witnesses. Walking back through the kitchen, he pushed open the freezer door once again.

The screaming stopped abruptly as Boggs fired several more rounds into the freezer, determined to silence any survivors. Only when he was certain the job was complete did he finally leave the scene.

Hargrave and Boggs exited the Jack in the Box into the warm Arizona night, their pockets containing less than three hundred dollars in cash and the personal effects of three people whose only crime had been showing up for work that evening.

Behind them, the restaurant sat silent and dark, its fluorescent lights casting an eerie glow over the empty kitchen. In the freezer at the back, three bodies lay still in the growing pool of blood, victims of a crime that had spiraled far beyond a simple robbery.

But in that freezer, something extraordinary was happening.

Despite catastrophic injuries, two of the three victims were not dead. Fausto Jimenez, though shot multiple times in the back, found the strength to move. Pain wracked his body as he crawled out of the freezer, leaving a trail of blood behind him.

Fausto dragged himself through the kitchen area, past the prep stations where he'd worked just hours earlier. Every movement sent waves of agony through his body, but he continued forward, driven by pure survival instinct.

Near the front counter, he found what he was looking for—a telephone. His hands slick with blood, he lifted the receiver and dialed 911. The connection went through, but Fausto's strength was failing rapidly. He collapsed near the phone before he could speak to an operator, but the call remained active, alerting emergency services that something was wrong.

Meanwhile, in the freezer, Betty Alvarado was fighting her own battle for survival. The bullets in her back had caused massive trauma, but some spark of life remained. Like Fausto, she began to move, crawling across the blood-slicked floor toward the freezer door.

Step by agonizing step, she made her way out of the freezer, through the cooler, and into the kitchen. Her vision blurred and her breathing came in short gasps, but she continued moving toward what she hoped was safety.

The back door of the restaurant became her goal. If she could just reach the outside, maybe someone would find her. Maybe help would come.

Betty pushed through the rear exit and collapsed in the parking area behind the Jack in the Box. Her body gave out, but she was outside now, visible to anyone who might happen by.

At 11:40 p.m., Luis Vargas pulled his car up to the drive-thru window of the Jack in the Box, expecting to place a late-night order. Instead, he heard something that chilled him to the bone—the sound of someone moaning in pain.

Vargas got out of his car and followed the sound to the back of the building. There, collapsed near the rear door, he found Betty Alvarado. She was still alive, though barely conscious and severely injured.

"What happened?" Vargas asked, kneeling beside her.

Betty's voice was weak, but she managed to speak. "Two," she whispered. "Two of them."

Vargas immediately called 911, reporting the injured woman and requesting emergency assistance. Within minutes, Mesa Police Officer Michael Beutal arrived at the scene.

Officer Beutal found Betty still conscious but fading fast. She repeated her crucial information to him: There had been two attackers inside the restaurant. Her words would prove vital to the investigation that was about to begin.

Despite the efforts of first responders, Betty Alvarado died from her injuries that night, but not before providing the key detail that would help investigators understand the scope of the crime.

When additional officers entered the Jack in the Box, they discovered a scene of horror. Fausto Jimenez lay dead near the telephone where he had made his desperate attempt to call for help. The open line to 911 told the story of his final heroic act.

In the freezer at the back of the restaurant, police found Kenneth Brown's body. Unlike his two coworkers, he had died almost immediately from his wounds. He had never moved from where he fell.

The crime scene told a clear story of execution-style murder. Multiple .45-caliber shell casings and bullet fragments were scattered across the freezer floor. Blood trails showed the paths Fausto and Betty had taken in their final, desperate attempts to escape.

The cash registers at the front had been pried open and emptied, though only loose change remained behind. The restaurant's safe was untouched, suggesting the perpetrators either didn't know about it or didn't have time to attempt to open it.

Mesa detectives began their investigation immediately, but they had little to go on beyond Betty's dying declaration about two attackers. The crime appeared to be a robbery gone horribly wrong, but the level of violence seemed excessive for such a small amount of money.

As investigators canvassed the area and interviewed other Jack in the Box employees, one name kept coming up: Christopher Hargrave, a former employee who had been fired just weeks earlier after problems with the cash register. Several workers mentioned that Hargrave had seemed angry about his termination, particularly toward Fausto Jimenez, who had reported the discrepancies that led to his firing.

The name Steve Boggs also surfaced as a known associate of Hargrave's. Both men had dropped off the radar since the night of the murders, which made them persons of interest in the investigation.

Two days after the killings, Detective Donald Vogel received a phone call that would crack the case wide open. Mrs. Driver, who owned a pawn shop with her husband and was the mother of Christopher Hargrave's girlfriend, had a troubling story to tell.

On May 21st, just two days after the Jack in the Box murders, Steve Boggs had appeared at their shop in an agitated state. He wanted to pawn a Taurus .45-caliber handgun, claiming he needed quick cash. The transaction had struck the Drivers as suspicious—Boggs seemed nervous and eager to complete the sale rapidly.

After Boggs left, Mr. Driver had examined the weapon more closely. Something about the timing and circumstances bothered him, especially given the news coverage of the restaurant murders. Mrs. Driver decided to contact the police.

When Detective Vogel arrived at the pawn shop to examine the weapon, he knew immediately that they had found something significant. The Taurus .45 was exactly the caliber of weapon that had been used in the Jack in the Box killings.

Forensic testing confirmed what Vogel suspected—the pawned handgun was indeed the murder weapon. Ballistics experts matched it to every shell casing and bullet fragment found at the crime scene. Even more damning, DNA analysis of the weapon's grip revealed Christopher Hargrave's genetic profile as a major contributor.

The evidence was overwhelming. Boggs had pawned the murder weapon, and Hargrave's DNA was all over it. On June 5th, Mesa Police brought Steve Boggs in for questioning.

After being read his Miranda rights, Boggs surprised investigators by waiving his right to remain silent. Over the course of a three-hour interrogation, he provided several conflicting stories about his whereabouts on the night of May 19.

When confronted with the ballistics evidence and the pawn shop records, Boggs's resistance crumbled. He eventually began to admit his involvement in the robbery and confessed to shooting the victims in the freezer.

But Boggs's most damning admission came later, in a letter he wrote to Detective Vogel after the interrogation. He wanted to "rid the world of a few needless illegals," referring to the Hispanic victims, and stated flatly that he "didn't feel sorry" for what he had done.

The robbery, investigators realized, had largely been a cover for a hate crime.

Boggs also provided information about Christopher Hargrave's whereabouts. After the murders, Hargrave had fled to a remote campsite in the Arizona desert, where he was heavily armed and preparing for what he expected to be a final confrontation with law enforcement.

On June 6, a SWAT team surrounded Hargrave's campsite and found him sleeping in a tent. Around him was an arsenal that included two handguns, a shotgun, two assault rifles, and boxes of ammunition. Also in his possession were documents related to a white supremacist organization called the Imperial Royal Guard, which Hargrave and Boggs had apparently founded together.

When awakened and arrested, Hargrave's first words to officers were chilling. He told them that "things would have been different" if they had caught him while he was awake, implying that he had been prepared to go down in a shootout.

The Imperial Royal Guard materials found at Hargrave's campsite painted a picture of two young men consumed by racial hatred. The organization was essentially a fantasy militia with grandiose titles—Boggs held the rank of "Chief of Staff" while Hargrave was "Assistant Chief of Staff." Their membership consisted mainly of themselves and their girl-friends.

The group's documents espoused white supremacist ideology and a hatred of racial minorities. Combined with the fact that all three victims at the Jack in the Box were people of color—Kenneth Brown was Native American, while Betty Alvarado and Fausto Jimenez were Hispanic—investigators concluded that racial hatred had been a primary motive for the murders.

———

The trials of Christopher Hargrave and Steve Boggs would reveal the full extent of their crimes and the ideology that drove them to murder three innocent people in the freezer of a fast-food restaurant. Both men were charged with three counts of first-degree murder, along with armed robbery, burglary, and kidnapping. The Maricopa County Attorney's Office sought the death penalty against both defendants.

Steve Boggs went to trial first in 2005. The evidence against him was overwhelming. Prosecutors presented his own videotaped confessions to the jury, in which he recounted forcing the victims into the freezer and methodically shooting them. They called Luis Vargas to testify about Beatriz Alvarado's dying declaration identifying two attackers. Forensic experts matched the recovered Taurus handgun to every shell casing and bullet fragment found at the crime scene.

Perhaps most damning was Boggs's own letter to Detective Vogel, in which he revealed his true motivation. He had written that he wanted to "rid the world of a few needless illegals," referring to what he assumed were undocumented immigrants. The twisted irony of his racist worldview became starkly apparent during the trial: Kenneth Brown, one of his victims, was Native American, making Brown's ancestors the original inhabitants of the continent, while Boggs himself was descended from European immigrants. In his warped ideology, Boggs had murdered the person with the greatest claim to being a native of this land.

Despite his defense team's attempts to highlight his troubled upbringing and mental health issues, including PTSD and bipolar disorder, the jury found Boggs guilty on all counts. During the penalty phase, they unanimously found three statutory aggravating factors for each murder: The crimes were committed for financial gain, in an especially cruel manner, and involved multiple victims. In May 2005, the jury sentenced Steve Boggs to death on each of the three murder counts.

Christopher Hargrave's trial followed in early 2006. Prosecutors presented equally compelling evidence against him: His DNA was on the murder weapon's grip, ATM security footage recorded him using Fausto Jimenez's bank card the night after the killings, and he'd had an arsenal of weapons found at his desert campsite. The Imperial Royal Guard documents seized from his possession painted a picture of a young man consumed by white supremacist hatred.

Unlike Boggs, Hargrave chose not to confess. His defense strategy was to admit involvement in the robbery while denying he personally killed anyone, attempting to pin the actual shootings solely on Boggs. He claimed he barely knew Boggs and had no knowledge that he planned to bring a gun or commit murder. However, the evidence contradicted his claims. Ballistics showed he had fired the weapon at least once in the freezer, and his heavily armed state when arrested suggested he was far from an unwitting accomplice.

Notably, Hargrave presented no mitigating evidence during his sentencing phase. He offered no apology, no explanation, and no plea for mercy. The jury found the same aggravating circumstances as in Boggs's case and, with nothing to weigh against them, sentenced Christopher Hargrave to death on all three murder counts in February 2006.

Both men appealed their convictions and death sentences through the Arizona court system. The Arizona Supreme Court upheld both convictions, finding that the evidence was overwhelming and the trials had been conducted fairly. The court specifically noted that the white supremacist evidence was properly admitted to establish motive, given that all three victims were minorities and racial epithets had been shouted during the killings.

As of today, both Christopher Hargrave and Steve Boggs remain on Arizona's death row at ASPC-Florence, their appeals continuing through state and federal courts. Neither has been executed, and both continue to serve their sentences more than twenty years after their horrific crimes shocked the community and demonstrated the deadly convergence of personal grievance and racist ideology.

The case would serve as a brutal reminder of the deadly potential of domestic extremism, where personal grievances and racist ideology could combine to produce unthinkable acts of violence. In the end, less than three hundred dollars and a twisted worldview had cost three people their lives, destroying countless others in the process.

CHAPTER 12

THE LONG WALK HOME

September 9, 1977, was supposed to be another typical Friday night for Mary Elizabeth Quigley. The seventeen-year-old Santa Clara High School senior had the kind of easy confidence that made people notice her when she walked into a room. Her blonde hair caught the light just right, and her smile had a warmth that drew classmates to her.

On this particular Friday evening, Mary was looking forward to a back-to-school keg party at a house near the corner of Market and Monroe Streets. It was the kind of gathering that defined teenage life in 1970s Santa Clara—casual, impromptu, and completely normal for kids their age. Mary lived with her mother, Janice Goodman, in a modest home not far from the high school where she was about to begin her senior year.

At seventeen, Mary embodied the freedom and optimism of her generation. She wore a fashionable jacket that reflected the era's embrace of self-expression. Her friend Brendan Murry often walked her home from school, and their tight-knit group of friends looked out for each other in the way that small-town teenagers always had.

The party plans came together the way most teenage gatherings did in 1977—word passed from friend to friend, rides were arranged, and everyone met up when the sun went down. Mary had secured transportation to the party with an acquaintance who promised to give her a ride on the back of his motorcycle.

When Mary arrived at the party, the house was already filled with familiar faces from Santa Clara High School. The music was loud, conversation flowed easily, and the atmosphere was relaxed and friendly. These were kids Mary had known for years—classmates, neighbors, friends of friends. The gathering had the comfortable feeling of a community where everyone knew everyone else.

As the evening wore on, the party continued with the rhythm of teenage social life. Groups formed and reformed, couples paired off, and the music provided a soundtrack for conversations and laughter. Mary was in her element, moving between groups of friends, catching up on summer activities, and looking forward to the upcoming school year. She had no way of knowing that someone at the party was watching her with intentions far darker than innocent teenage socializing.

The night took an unexpected turn when Mary's promised ride decided to leave early. Her motorcycle-riding acquaintance departed the party without telling her, leaving Mary stranded without transportation home. It was the kind of inconsiderate behavior that happened at teenage parties, usually resulting in nothing more than irritation and the need to find alternative arrangements.

Mary faced a decision that thousands of teenagers make every weekend: how to get home safely. In 1977 Santa Clara, the options seemed straightforward and relatively harmless. She could ask another friend for a ride, call her mother for a pickup, or simply walk to a nearby friend's house. The streets of Santa Clara felt safe to teenagers who had grown up there, and walking alone at night didn't carry the same sense of danger that it would in later decades.

Around 11:45 p.m., witnesses saw Mary leaving the party on foot, walking alone into the warm September night. She was headed toward the house of a friend who lived nearby, taking what would have been a familiar route through War Memorial Park. It was a walk that Mary had probably made dozens of times before, alone or with friends. The path would take her across the park grounds, past the athletic fields of her own high school, and toward the residential streets on the other side.

Mary walked into the darkness, carrying herself with the same confidence that had made her so popular at school. She had no way of knowing that her decision to walk home alone would set in motion a chain of events that would haunt the Santa Clara community for the next three decades.

———

The morning of September 10, 1977, began like any other Saturday for the groundskeeper at War Memorial Park. During his morning rounds, he noticed something unusual near the chain-link fence that separated the park from some nearby apartments. From a distance, it appeared to be an object pressed against the fence, but the early morning light made it difficult to see clearly.

For hours, the groundskeeper continued with his other duties, the strange object at the fence nagging at the back of his mind. Something about its shape and position seemed wrong, but he couldn't quite put his finger on what was bothering him. As the morning progressed and the light improved, however, his unease grew stronger.

Around noon, with his other tasks completed, the groundskeeper decided to investigate the object more closely. As he approached the fence, what he saw made him stop in his tracks and sent a chill down his spine. The object wasn't debris or discarded clothing—it was a human body.

Mary Quigley hung from the chain-link fence, suspended by the sash of her own jacket. She was nude except for her socks and shoes, her clothing scattered across the ground in front of the fence. The scene was both horrific and surreal, transforming the familiar park into something unrecognizable and terrifying.

Within minutes, Santa Clara Police and emergency personnel arrived at the scene, their faces grim as they took in the brutal reality of what had happened. The park was immediately cordoned off, yellow tape fluttering in the breeze as investigators began the careful process of documenting what was clearly a homicide.

The crime scene told a story of unimaginable violence. Evidence suggested that Mary had been attacked approximately 30 feet away from the fence, stripped of her clothing, and then dragged to where her body was found. Her underwear was discovered inside-out, dangling from one ankle, while her outer clothing was scattered across the field like discarded remnants of a life cut short.

The medical examiner's preliminary assessment painted an even more disturbing picture: Mary had been raped and strangled. There were no defensive wounds on her hands or arms, suggesting that she had been overpowered quickly and brutally. The positioning of her body—hung from the fence in a deliberately degrading display—indicated that this was more than just a violent crime. Someone had taken time to stage the scene, to make a statement that went beyond the act of murder itself.

The location of the crime scene was particularly chilling. Mary's body was found approximately 300 yards from where she had last been seen leaving the party, as well as about 100 yards from the path through the park that she would logically have taken to reach her friend's house. This suggested that the attack had occurred during her walk home, possibly by someone who had followed her from the party or encountered her by chance in the park.

As word of the discovery spread through Santa Clara, the community was plunged into shock and fear. Mary Quigley was not just another teenager—she was someone's daughter, classmate, and friend. She represented every parent's worst fear about the vulnerability of their children, and every teenager's nightmare about the dangers that could lurk in familiar places.

The crime scene investigation continued throughout the day, with detectives carefully collecting evidence and photographing every detail. They cut out the section of the fence where Mary's body had been found, preserving it as evidence. Every fiber, every trace of biological material, every fingerprint was catalogued and stored, representing pieces of a puzzle that investigators hoped would eventually lead them to Mary's killer.

Detective work in 1977 bore little resemblance to the high-tech forensic investigations that would become common in later decades. The Santa Clara Police Department responded to Mary Quigley's murder with the tools and techniques available at the time: witness interviews, fingerprint analysis, and traditional detective work that relied heavily on developing leads through human connections and painstaking police work.

The initial investigation focused on retracing Mary's final hours and identifying everyone who had been at the party on Monroe and Market Streets. Detectives methodically interviewed party guests, asking about Mary's mood, her interactions with other attendees, and whether anyone had noticed anything unusual about the evening. They were searching for any detail, no matter how small, that might point toward a suspect or provide insight into who might have followed Mary when she left the party.

The interviews revealed a picture of a typical teenage gathering with all the usual dynamics. Mary had been her normal, friendly self, talking with various groups of friends and enjoying the social atmosphere. Several witnesses confirmed that she had left the party alone around 11:45 p.m., walking in the direction of her friend's house. No one reported seeing anyone follow her or noticing any unusual behavior from other party guests.

Still, the investigators knew that someone at that party might hold the key to solving Mary's murder. Someone had seen her leave. Someone might have decided to follow her. Someone might have noticed a classmate acting strangely or disappearing around the same time Mary did. The answers were there, buried somewhere in the memories of teenagers who had been focused on having fun rather than watching for signs of potential violence.

Detectives also canvassed the neighborhood around War Memorial Park, knocking on doors and looking for residents who might have seen or heard something during the critical hours between Mary's departure from the party and the discovery of her body. This process yielded some intriguing information that would trouble investigators.

A neighbor reported being awakened by barking dogs sometime between 10 p.m. and midnight. According to this witness, she had looked out her window and seen what appeared to be four men speaking to a young woman near the area where Mary's body would later be found. The interaction had seemed aggressive, but when a car full of girls had stopped and asked the young woman if she wanted to leave with them, she'd reportedly said she was fine. The witness had gone back to bed, not thinking much more about the incident until she heard about Mary's murder.

This account was both tantalizing and maddening for investigators. If the witness had indeed seen Mary's final moments, it suggested that multiple people might have been involved in the crime. However, the witness had observed the scene from a distance in poor lighting conditions, making it impossible to provide detailed descriptions of the individuals involved. Had she witnessed Mary's murder, or had she seen an unrelated incident? The uncertainty was agonizing.

The biological evidence collected at the crime scene represented both the best hope for solving the case and a source of enormous frustration for investigators. Semen samples had been recovered from Mary's body, providing clear evidence that a sexual assault had occurred. However, the technology to analyze DNA and match it to specific individuals was still years away from practical application in criminal investigations.

In 1977, the most sophisticated biological testing available involved blood typing and other basic serological techniques that could narrow down potential suspects but couldn't definitively identify them. The semen samples were carefully preserved and stored in the crime laboratory's evidence room, representing a potential breakthrough that investigators knew might someday be possible, but which they couldn't access with current technology.

As the investigation continued into its second and third weeks, detectives found themselves with plenty of evidence but no clear path toward identifying a suspect. They had a detailed understanding of Mary's final hours, comprehensive crime scene documentation, and preserved biological evidence, but no obvious leads that pointed toward any particular individual. The case was becoming every investigator's nightmare.

————

As the 1970s turned into the 1980s, Mary Quigley's murder joined the growing ranks of unsolved cases that haunted American police departments. The initial burst of investigative activity had yielded a comprehensive understanding of Mary's final hours and detailed crime scene analysis, but no breakthrough that could lead to an arrest.

The case took on the characteristics that would define it for the next three decades: strong physical evidence that couldn't yet be fully exploited, a crime that appeared to have been committed by someone familiar with the victim or the area, and a community desperately seeking answers that the available investigative tools couldn't provide.

What made Mary Quigley's case unusual wasn't just its brutality, but the sustained effort by her friends and family to keep it alive. As the years passed and other crimes captured headlines, Mary's loved ones refused to let her case fade into obscurity. Michael Knoy became particularly dedicated to this cause, establishing a memorial website where he posted information about the case and offered rewards for information that might lead to the killer's identification.

Brendan Murry, who had often walked Mary home from school, carried the weight of the unsolved case throughout his adult life. He would later describe feeling "haunted" by Mary's murder—by questions about what might have happened if he had been with her that night, if different decisions had been made about transportation from the party.

The dedication of Mary's friends and family played a crucial role in keeping pressure on law enforcement to continue working on the case. Their persistence ensured that Mary's murder didn't become just another cold case file gathering dust in a storage room. Instead, it remained a visible reminder of the community's demand for justice and resolution.

———

As forensic science began to advance through the 1980s and 1990s, investigators periodically revisited Mary's case, hoping that new techniques might yield fresh insights. Blood typing and other serological tests were applied to the preserved evidence, providing some additional information.

However, it was nothing that could point definitively toward a specific suspect.

The case took on a rhythm that characterized many long-term investigations: periods of intense activity when new leads emerged, followed by stretches of relative quiet when all available avenues had been exhausted. Each new detective assigned to the case would spend time familiarizing themselves with the details, looking for connections that previous investigators might have missed.

One detective who became particularly invested was Sergeant Ted Keech, who inherited the investigation in the late 1980s. Keech brought fresh eyes to the evidence and conducted additional interviews with witnesses and potential suspects. Despite his dedicated efforts, the case remained frustratingly elusive.

Throughout the 1990s, DNA analysis was becoming increasingly sophisticated and affordable. Cases that had been unsolvable for decades were suddenly being cracked through genetic testing that could identify perpetrators with unprecedented accuracy. By the late 1990s, Mary's case was still cold, but technology was finally catching up to the evidence that had been preserved for more than two decades. Thus, cold case units were being established in police departments across the country, specifically to take advantage of these new capabilities.

California was at the forefront of these developments, particularly with the passage of Proposition 69 in 2004, which dramatically expanded the collection of DNA samples from convicted criminals. The law required DNA collection from all convicted felons, creating a much larger pool of genetic profiles that could be searched when evidence from unsolved cases was tested.

For Mary's friends and family, these developments represented new hope that her case might finally be solved.

———

Detective Sergeant Wahid Kazem had spent considerable
time reviewing cold cases during his tenure with the Santa
Clara Police Department. In 2005, with the expansion of
DNA databases beginning to show dramatic results in other
jurisdictions, he made a decision that would ultimately solve
one of Santa Clara's most notorious unsolved murders.

Kazem decided to resubmit evidence from Mary Quigley's
1977 murder for comprehensive DNA analysis. The decision
wasn't taken lightly. Cold case investigations require significant resources, and there was no guarantee that the nearly
thirty-year-old evidence would yield usable DNA profiles.
Biological evidence degrades over time, and the storage
conditions in 1977 weren't necessarily optimal for long-term
preservation of genetic material.

However, the evidence from Mary's case had been carefully
preserved by the Santa Clara County Crime Lab. The fore-
sight of the original investigators in properly storing the
biological samples would prove to be crucial decades later.
When the evidence was submitted for DNA analysis, technicians were able to extract clear, usable genetic profiles from
the semen samples collected at the crime scene nearly three
decades earlier.

The profiles were entered into the Combined DNA Index
System (CODIS), the national DNA database that allows law
enforcement agencies to search for matches across multiple
jurisdictions. The system automatically compares new
profiles against hundreds of thousands of genetic profiles

already in the database, looking for exact matches that would indicate the same individual was responsible for multiple crimes.

For months, the DNA profiles sat in the system, waiting for a match that might never come. Then, on December 27, 2006, Detective Kazem received a phone call that would change everything, finally bringing closure to one of Santa Clara's most haunting unsolved cases.

The crime laboratory informed him that they had found a match in the database. The DNA from Mary Quigley's 1977 murder matched a profile belonging to a Santa Clara resident—someone who had been living in the same community where Mary had been killed, someone who had been walking the same streets and shopping in the same stores while Mary's friends and family wondered who had taken her life.

In addition, the match was not just close or even probable—it was definitive. The odds against the DNA belonging to someone other than the suspect were calculated in the millions to one. After nearly 30 years of uncertainty, investigators finally had conclusive proof of who had killed Mary Quigley.

The name that appeared on the computer screen would shock everyone involved in the case: Richard Armand Archibeque, a 47-year-old Santa Clara resident who had been required to submit a DNA sample because of a previous criminal conviction.

Richard Archibeque

The revelation of Richard Archibeque's identity sent shock-waves through the Santa Clara Police Department and would forever change how the community viewed Mary Quigley's murder. Richard wasn't a stranger who had passed through town in 1977—he had been Mary's own classmate at Santa Clara High School.

Born January 26, 1959, Richard was eighteen years old at the time of Mary's murder, and he had been at the same party on Monroe and Market Streets where Mary had spent her final evening. While Mary moved easily through social circles, comfortable with everyone from the popular kids to the shy ones, Richard had remained on the periphery, a quiet and awkward presence that few people noticed or remembered.

Richard was physically small—just 5'1" and ninety pounds at the time of the murder—with long hair that fell across his face. What made him most distinctive was his glass eye, which he needed after a BB gun accident with his cousin when he was fourteen. Classmates would later recall him as strange and antisocial, a loner who didn't fit in with any particular group. Some remembered the disturbing way he would sometimes remove his glass eye in class, causing other students to look away in discomfort.

The most chilling aspect of Richard's identification was what it revealed about his behavior in the aftermath of Mary's murder. He had returned to school that fall as if nothing had happened, sitting in the same classes where Mary's friends grieved her loss, walking the same hallways where memorial ribbons had been tied, and blending into the background while the community reeled from the shock of her brutal death.

To his classmates, Richard appeared to be dealing with Mary's death the same way everyone else was—with shock and sadness. No one suspected that the awkward boy with the glass eye had any connection to the horrific crime that had shattered their sense of safety. His distinctive appearance and small stature actually worked in his favor, as many people couldn't imagine him being capable of such brutal violence.

But what investigators discovered about Richard's activities after Mary's murder painted a disturbing picture of a young man who had been emboldened by getting away with killing.

The more serious escalation came in July 1979, when Richard committed a crime that would prove chillingly similar to Mary's murder. He attacked a sixteen-year-old girl on Lafayette Street near the Southern Pacific Railroad overpass, using methods that seemed to follow an identical playbook. Richard placed a rag over the girl's mouth, choked her, dragged her across a field, undressed her, and raped her near a fence.

This attack was solved relatively quickly because an alert detective noticed similarities between the Lafayette Street assault and other incidents. The pattern of escalating violence and the specific methods used in the attack provided enough evidence to convict Richard of rape, resulting in a three-year state prison sentence.

The similarities between Richard's known crimes and Mary's murder were so striking that they appeared to represent his signature approach to violence: young women attacked while walking alone, choking and dragging, sexual assault, and the recurring element of fences as locations for his crimes. The methods were too specific and numerous to be coincidental.

Richard's criminal history also revealed potential psychological motivations for his violence against women. In interviews with probation officers, he expressed resentment about a failed relationship where his girlfriend's father had forced her to break up with him because he was Hispanic. This sense of rejection and anger toward women, combined with his social awkwardness and physical insecurities, may have contributed to violent fantasies that culminated in Mary's murder.

After serving three years in prison for the 1979 rape, Richard was released in 1982 and returned to Santa Clara, where he attempted to build what appeared to be a normal life. He worked first at Pizza Hut and later as a handyman for his mother's rental properties. Richard married and divorced, raised a daughter, and lived quietly in a bungalow owned by his mother near the Santa Clara town center, less than a mile from War Memorial Park, where he had murdered Mary Quigley.

For more than two decades, Richard had been hiding in plain sight, living in the same community where he had committed his most serious crime. Every day, he could see reminders of what he had done, yet he maintained his facade of normalcy while Mary's friends and family continued their desperate search for answers about who had killed her.

————

On December 27, 2006, the same day the DNA match was confirmed, Santa Clara detectives moved swiftly to arrest Richard Archibeque. There was no delay, no extended surveillance, and no complex investigation to build additional evidence. The DNA match was so conclusive that it provided sufficient probable cause for immediate arrest.

Richard was taken into custody at his mother's bungalow. Neighbors watched in shock as police cars surrounded the modest home and led away the man they had known as a quiet, unremarkable member of the community.

The arrest brought immediate relief to Mary's mother, Janice Goodman, who had waited twenty-nine years for this moment. For Mary's friends, the arrest represented both closure and a profoundly disturbing revelation. Brendan Murry and Michael Knoy, along with other classmates who had maintained their vigil for justice, suddenly had to confront the reality that they had known Mary's killer. They had walked the same hallways, attended the same classes, and been present at the same party where Mary had spent her final hours.

The shock of learning that Richard Archibeque—the strange, awkward boy with the glass eye—had been responsible for Mary's brutal murder forced them to question everything they thought they knew about their high school years. How had they missed the signs? Had there been warning signals that they had failed to recognize? The realization that evil could hide behind such an unremarkable facade was deeply unsettling.

Richard was charged with first-degree murder, with a special circumstance allegation of murder committed during the course of a rape. This special circumstance made him eligible for either the death penalty or life in prison without the possibility of parole if convicted.

———

In early 2009, more than thirty-one years after Mary's murder, the trial of Richard Archibeque began at the San Jose Hall of Justice. The courtroom became a gathering place for people whose lives had been forever changed by Mary's death, bringing together friends, family members, investigators, and community members who had followed the case for decades.

The prosecution, led by Deputy District Attorney James Gibbons-Shapiro, presented a methodical and devastating case. They called twenty-five witnesses during the trial, including many of Mary's friends and classmates, who testified about the party, Mary's departure, and the shock that followed the discovery of her body. These witnesses, now adults in their late forties, had to recall events from their teenage years, but their memories had been preserved by the trauma of losing someone they cared about.

The testimony painted a picture of Mary as a vibrant young woman whose life had been cut short by senseless violence. Michael Knoy, who had maintained the memorial website for Mary throughout the years, broke down in tears when describing her as "magical" and explaining how her murder had affected their entire group of friends.

Both Knoy and Murry also testified about their memories of Richard Archibeque as a strange, awkward classmate who didn't fit in with other students. Murry recalled Richard's disturbing classroom behavior: "He was a loner. He just didn't fit in. In eighth grade, he would be sitting in class and pull out his eyeball and play with it on his desk. He already had a stigma before high school."

The centerpiece of the prosecution's case was the DNA evidence. Expert witnesses from the Santa Clara County Crime Laboratory explained how genetic profiles had been extracted from biological evidence collected in 1977, as well as how those profiles had been matched to Richard Archibeque with mathematical certainty.

The prosecution also presented compelling evidence of Richard's pattern of criminal behavior, including his 1978 assault and 1979 rape conviction. These crimes demonstrated a clear escalation of violence against women and showed methods that were strikingly similar to those used in Mary's murder. The prosecution argued that Richard had developed a signature approach to attacking women that culminated in Mary's death.

The defense strategy, led by Deputy Public Defender Charles Gillan, proved difficult to execute effectively. Facing overwhelming DNA evidence, Gillan argued that Richard had engaged in consensual sex with Mary up to seventy-two hours before her murder. He claimed she had subsequently been killed by "drugged-up thugs" from the party who had since died.

However, this theory faced significant problems. No evidence suggested any romantic relationship between Richard and Mary, no witnesses testified to seeing them together at the party, and the absence of semen in Mary's underwear contradicted the theory of recent consensual sexual activity. The defense also argued that Richard was too small to have committed the crime, but the prosecution countered that his size could have been an advantage in surprising and overpowering an unsuspecting victim.

Throughout the trial, Richard's seventeen-year-old daughter attended the proceedings, maintaining her belief in her father's innocence. She had been born after Richard's release from prison and had known him only as a quiet, dedicated father. The revelation of his violent past and the evidence of his guilt in Mary's murder were devastating to her understanding of who her father was.

After three days of deliberation, the jury returned with its verdict on March 2, 2009. They found Richard Archibeque guilty of first-degree murder in the death of Mary Quigley. However, they rejected the special circumstance allegation of murder during rape, which meant that Richard would not be eligible for the death penalty.

―――――

On March 27, 2009, Richard Archibeque was sentenced to seven years to life in prison. While this represented the resolution that Mary's family and friends had sought for more than three decades, the sentence also highlighted one of the complexities of prosecuting decades-old crimes.

The seven-year minimum sentence reflected the legal standards that existed in 1977, when the crime was committed, rather than the harsher penalties that would have applied under modern law. In 1977, California's sentencing guidelines for first-degree murder were significantly more lenient than they would become in subsequent decades. The "seven to life" sentence meant that Richard could theoretically be eligible for parole after serving just seven years, though the brutal nature of his crime and his pattern of violence against women made such an outcome highly unlikely.

Had Richard been sentenced under contemporary guidelines that existed at the time of his 2009 conviction, he would have received a minimum of 25 years to life. The disparity highlighted the evolution of California's criminal justice system and society's changing views about appropriate punishment for violent crimes. For Mary's family and friends, the relatively light minimum sentence was a source of frustration, but it also represented the formal acknowledgment of Richard's guilt that had been missing from their lives since 1977.

———

The conviction was appealed, as is routine in serious criminal cases, but the 6th District Court of Appeal upheld Richard's conviction in 2010. The appellate court called the prosecution's case "more than adequate" and rejected Richard's arguments that there was insufficient evidence to support his murder conviction. The appeal decision ensured that Richard would remain in prison and that Mary's family would not have to endure another trial.

The case had lasting impacts on the Santa Clara community. War Memorial Park, where Mary's body had been found, became a place of memorial rather than just a crime scene. A memorial plaque was placed at the site, although friends and classmates campaigned for further tributes to honor her memory.

Richard Archibeque remains in prison, eligible for parole hearings but facing the reality that his crime and pattern of violence against women make release extremely unlikely.

Online Appendix

Visit my website for additional photos and videos pertaining to the cases in this book:

http://TrueCrimeCaseHistories.com/vol19/

More books by Jason Neal

Looking for more?? I am constantly adding new volumes of True Crime Case Histories. The series **can be read in any order,** and all books are available in paperback, hardcover, and audiobook.

Check out the complete series on Amazon series at:

https://geni.us/JasonNeal

As my way of saying "Thank you" for reading, I'm giving away a FREE True Crime e-book I think you'll enjoy.

https://TrueCrimeCaseHistories.com

Just visit the link above to let me know where to send your free book!

THANK YOU!

Thank you for reading this Volume of True Crime Case Histories. I truly hope you enjoyed it. If you did, I would be sincerely grateful if you would take a few minutes to write a review for me on Amazon using the link below.

https://geni.us/TrueCrime19

I'd also like to encourage you to sign up for my email list for updates, discounts, and freebies on future books! I promise I'll make it worth your while with future freebies.

http://truecrimecasehistories.com

And please take a moment and follow me on Amazon.

http://amazon.com/author/jason-neal/

Thanks so much,

Jason Neal

ABOUT THE AUTHOR

Jason Neal is a Best-Selling American True Crime Author living in Hawaii with his Turkish-British wife. Jason started his writing career in the late eighties as a music industry publisher and wrote his first true crime collection in 2019.

As a boy growing up in the eighties just south of Seattle, Jason became interested in true crime stories after hearing the news of the Green River Killer so close to his home. Over the subsequent years, he would read everything he could get his hands on about true crime and serial killers.

As he approached 50, Jason began to assemble stories of the crimes that have fascinated him most throughout his life. He's especially obsessed by cases solved by sheer luck, amazing police work, and groundbreaking technology like early DNA cases and, more recently, reverse genealogy.

Printed in Dunstable, United Kingdom